Black
white
gray
cyan
magenta
yellow

Lars Bang Larsen

Simon Dybbroe Møller

Jo Baer
Walter De Maria
Jim Dine
Donald Judd
Gary Kuehn
Robert Morris
Bruce Nauman
Robert Ryman
Cy Twombly
Andy Warhol

EIN WERK MIT VIELEN DIMENSIONEN
Simon Dybbroe Møllers <u>Black, White and Gray (Cyan, Magenta and Yellow)</u>

Lars Bang Larsen

1.
Donald Judd war von den Verdiensten der Ausstellung <u>Black, White and Gray</u> nicht überzeugt. Seine Ausstellungsbesprechung eröffnete er mit der Salve: »Schwarz, Weiß und Grau ist, wie Schwarzweiß, ein mageres Thema.«[I] Mehr als 40 Jahre später schafft Simon Dybbroe Møller eine Arbeit, mit der er dem Meister des Minimalismus widerspricht, oder – je nach Perspektive – dessen Urteil durch die Hinzufügung von ein paar Farben vervollständigt. Es war wohl nicht Judds Absicht, die Tradition der monochromen Malerei mit ihren utopischen Zukunftsentwürfen abzulehnen, die zur Zeit seiner Ausstellungskritik Anfang der 1960er Jahre noch immer Bestand hatten. Vielmehr konnte er nicht absehen, in welchem Umfang binäre Systeme – der Farbkombination schwarz/weiss nicht unähnlich – unsere Zukunft mittels ihrer Rolle in der Informationstechnologie definieren sollten. Er konnte es nicht vorausahnen und solch detaillierte Ausflüge in den Einfallsreichtum der Zukunft waren in seiner künstlerischen Praxis nicht angelegt. Im Unterschied hierzu würde Simon Dybbroe Møller mit Sicherheit nichts dagegen haben, wenn wir seine Arbeiten als Zeitmaschinen bezeichneten, könnte man doch ihr primäres Anliegen als das der Dimensionalität beschreiben.
        Dybbroe Møllers Arbeit <u>Black, White and Gray (Cyan, Magenta and Yellow)</u> aus dem Jahr 2006, ist eine Tapete von ungefähr 30 Metern Länge und so hoch wie der Raum, in dem sie angebracht wird. Sie besteht aus über 2000 einzelnen DIN-A4-Blättern, die man als große Pixel eines fotografischen Bildes verstehen kann, das mittels Computer

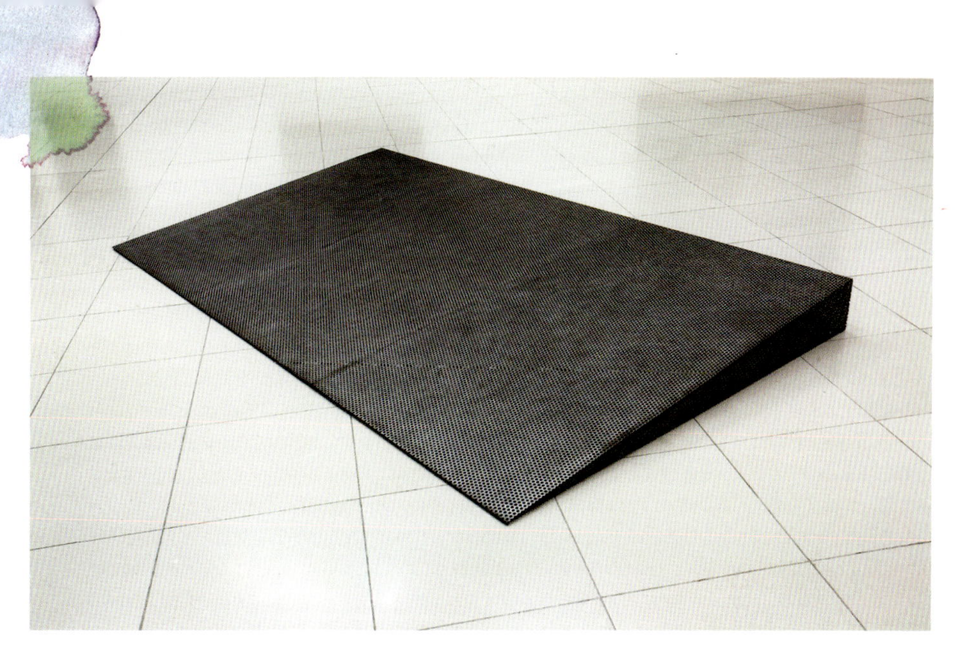

Donald Judd
<u>Untitled</u>, 1965/68

in dieser Form aufgeteilt wurde. In ihrer Gesamtheit
zeigen die Blätter eine Installationsansicht der Malerei-
und Skulpturenausstellung Black, White and Gray, die
von Samuel Wagstaff Jr. kuratiert und im Januar 1964
im Atheneum Museum in Wadsworth, Connecticut, eröffnet
wurde. Black, White and Gray wird zuweilen als die erste
Ausstellung der Minimal Art bezeichnet. Zwar ist dies
eine fragliche Behauptung, aber die Ausstellung war mit
Sicherheit darin erfolgreich, dem Durchschnittsbesucher
einen strengen, minimalistischen Stil näher zu bringen.[II]
Das Bild, das Simon Dybbroe Møllers Tapete zugrunde liegt,
ist aus zwei Installationsansichten zusammengesetzt, um
ein Panorama des Hauptraums der Ausstellung zu liefern.
Auf dem Foto sieht man unter anderem Arbeiten von
Robert Morris, Tony Smith, Anne Truitt und James Lee
Byars, die im Atrium des Museums um eine manieristische
Brunnenskulptur von Pietro Francavilla aus dem frühen
17. Jahrhundert herum angeordnet sind, einer Venus mit
Nymphe und Satyr (um 1600).

Doch besitzt die Tapete einen seltsamen Ausschlag,
gleich einem untoten Bild mit dem Gesicht eines Zombies
oder einer von Grünspan-Patina überlagerten Bronze-
skulptur, die jahrzehntelang in einem Park stand. Die
Geschichte dahinter ist die folgende: Als Simon Dybbroe
Møller im Sommer 2006 im Mittelmeer segeln war, hatte
er ein Blatt Papier mit ein paar Adressen dabei, das
er in einem Internet Café ausgedruckt hatte. Als er es
nach einigen Tagen aus seiner Hosentasche nahm, waren
die schwarzen Buchstaben von einem »psychedelischen
Farbschleier«, wie er es nannte, umgeben, weil sie feucht
geworden waren.[III] Einen ähnlichen Prozess nutzt er für
Black, White and Gray (Cyan, Magenta and Yellow). Die
Ausdrucke sind schwarzweiß aber im CMYK-Modus gedruckt.
Klebt man sie mit Tapetenkleister auf die Wand, so lösen
die Chemikalien und die Feuchtigkeit des Kleisters das
Blau, Magenta und Gelb aus der schwarzen Tinte heraus.

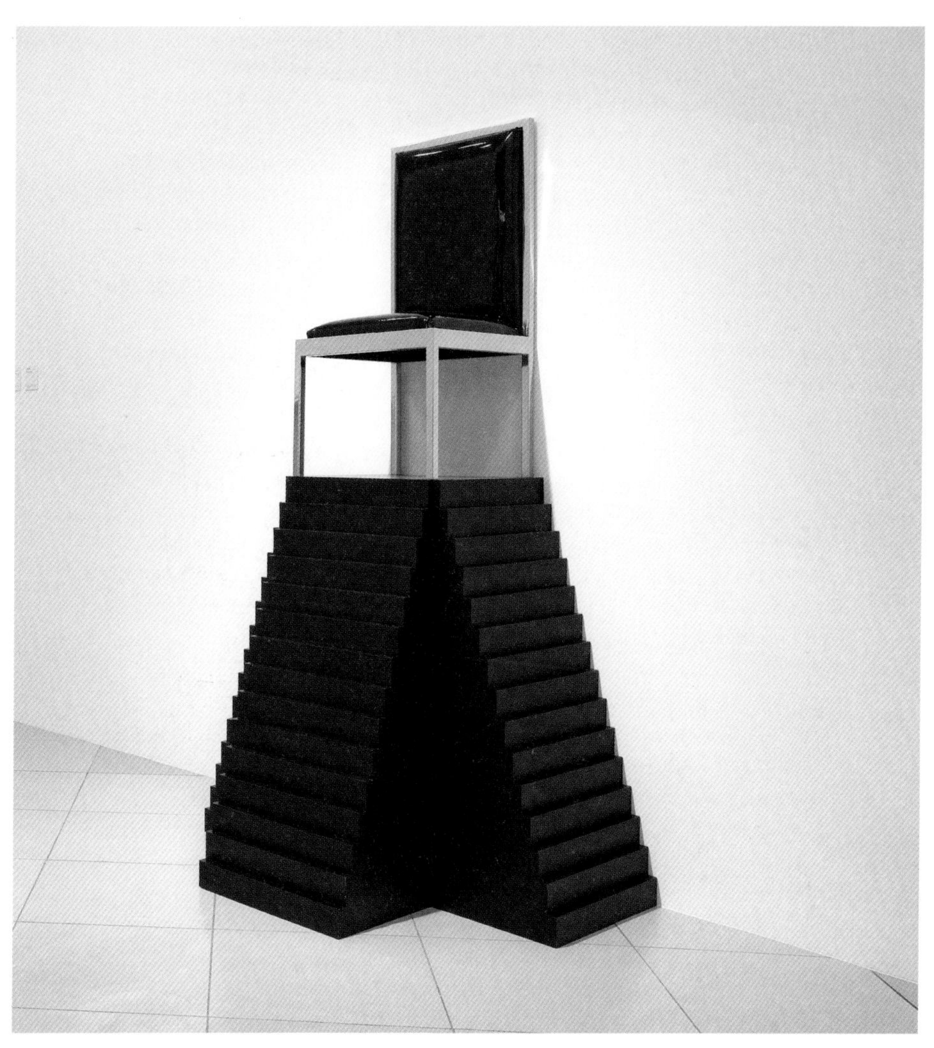

Walter De Maria
<u>Pyramid Chair</u>, 1966

Auf diese Weise werden den ›mageren‹ Schwarz-, Weiß- und
Grautönen des Fotos Farben hinzugefügt. Diese Farben
machen die gestischen Bewegungen der Kleisterquaste
sichtbar, mittels derer die Blätter aufgeklebt wurden.
Die im Bild dokumentierten ursprünglichen Strukturen
erscheinen unter einem Schleier allegorischer Opazität.

Auch Zeitmaschinen sind bekannt dafür, überraschende
Lichtschattierungen und -täuschungen hervorzurufen. Dieser
kosmische Ausblick im Zeitraffer bot sich auch dem Zeit-
reisenden von H.G. Wells, als er sich in den Sattel seiner
Maschine aus Nickel, Eisen und Bergkristall schwang,
den Vorwärtshebel umlegte und sich auf die Reise in die
Zukunft begab:

Als ich die Geschwindigkeit vermehrte, folgte die
Nacht dem Tage wie das Schlagen eines schwarzen
Flügels. Dann schien die dunkle Andeutung des
Laboratoriums von mir abzufallen, und ich sah die
Sonne über den Himmel hüpfen: jede Minute sprang
sie hinüber, und jede Minute war ein Tag. Ich
dachte mir, das Laboratorium sei zerstört und ich
sei in die freie Luft hinausgekommen. Ich hatte
eine dunkle Empfindung des Stürzens, aber ich ging
schon zu schnell, um mir noch sich bewegender Dinge
bewusst zu werden. Die langsamste Schnecke, die
jemals kroch, raste zu schnell an mir vorbei. Die
blinkende Folge von Dunkelheit und Licht war fürs
Auge außerordentlich schmerzhaft. Dann sah ich in
den dunklen Intervallen den Mond schnell durch seine
Viertel spinnen, vom Neumond bis zum Vollmond, und
dunkel sah ich die kreisenden Sterne. Dann wurde,
als ich immer noch an Geschwindigkeit gewann, das
Zucken von Tag und Nacht zu einer kontinuierlichen
Grauheit; der Himmel nahm eine wundervolle Tiefe des
Blaus an, eine glänzende, leuchtende Farbe gleich der
des frühen Zwielichts; die springende Sonne wurde

Jim Dine
<u>Black Bathroom #1</u>, 1962

> ein Feuerstreif, ein glänzender Bogen im Raum; der
> Mond ein schwächeres, fluktuierendes Band; und von
> den Sternen konnte ich nichts mehr sehen als hin und
> wieder einen helleren Kreis, der im Blau aufzitterte.[IV]

Eine ähnliche Störung im Lauf der Zeit erscheint bei Dybbroe Møller. Der Titel seiner Einzelausstellung im Künstlerhaus Bremen 2006 Letter From the New World to the Old World, in der Black, White and Gray (Cyan, Magenta and Yellow) zum ersten Mal zu sehen war, bezog sich vorgeblich auf einen aus den USA nach Europa geschickten Brief. Aber was wäre, wenn diese Bewegung zeitlich und nicht geographisch gedacht wäre, sich die ›neue Welt‹ nicht auf einen anderen Ort, sondern auf eine andere Zeit bezöge? Was für Briefe würden wir erhalten? Dybbroe Møllers Arbeiten suchen existierende Dinge mit Fragen und Hypothesen heim, die die Gegenwart selbst nicht generiert. Das ist weder eine Heilung der Geschichte noch ein Verlangen nach der Vergangenheit. Vielmehr handelt es sich bei Dybbroe Møllers Arbeiten um seltsame Bilder und Objekte, die es so nie gab, die aber mögliche Resultate unserer Vergangenheit sein könnten oder kristallisierte Ergebnisse einer sich an die Vergangenheit anschließenden Entwicklung; Dinge, die es gegeben haben wird, wenn wir unserem Begehren nach Zukunft bis zum Ende folgen. Es geht also nicht um das Verändern der Vergangenheit mit dem Ziel die Zukunft zu verändern, sondern darum, in die Zukunft einzugreifen, um die Art und Weise zu verändern, wie die Vergangenheit in der Gegenwart erscheint.

Ich glaube, es ist dieses Enthüllen der Ruinen möglicher Zukunftsszenarien, diese ›Archäologie der Zukunft‹, wie man mit Frederic Jameson sagen könnte, mit der sich Dybbroe Møller beschäftigt.[V] Es wird häufig behauptet, seine Arbeiten drehten sich um den Modernismus und es stimmt, dass dies die Epoche ist, die er gewöhnlich aufsucht, um Rohmaterial zu finden. Was er zu Tage befördert,

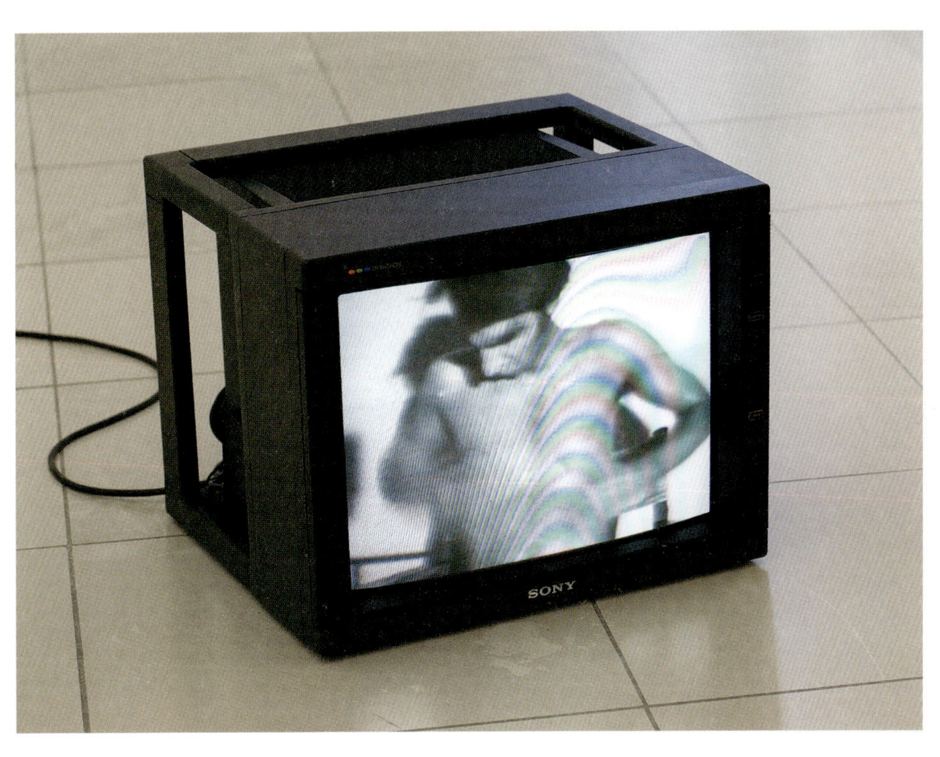

Bruce Nauman
<u>From Flesh to White to Black to Flesh</u>, 1968

sind aber viel eher die Energien des Modernismus und
dessen Bestreben, die Welt von Morgen zu erdenken, als
der Modernismus selbst, wie er stattgefunden hat. Heute,
in einer globalen Kultur, die vor allem damit beschäftigt
ist, sich zu reproduzieren, ist die Zukunft eine so
bedrohte Ressource wie Öl, intakte Natur und sauberes
Trinkwasser. Um dieser misslichen Lage Widerstand zu
leisten, benutzt Dybbroe Møller den Modernismus, um
danach Ausschau zu halten, was von der Zukunft übrig
geblieben ist. (Von Künstlern wie David Maljkovic, Goshka
Macuga, Maria Loboda und Paul Sietsema, um einige seiner
Generation zu nennen, könnte man sagen, dass sie ein
ähnliches Anliegen verfolgen.)

2.

Mit dem Mittel der Farbe eröffnet <u>Black, White and Gray
(Cyan, Magenta and Yellow)</u> ein Kaleidoskop von Ab-
lagerungen: Schichten von Geschichte, die abgezogen,
verschoben und transformiert werden können, wie Licht
durch ein Prisma. Denn Farbe tendiert dazu, Realität
durcheinander zu bringen und in andere Dimensionen über-
gehen zu lassen. Sofern sie keinem Objekt subsumiert ist,
bringt die Opazität der Farbe die Sprache und das Denken
als Werkzeuge in Verlegenheit, mittels derer wir das Reale
festnageln und uns an ihm festhalten. Realität durch Farbe
weich und formbar wiederzugeben war zweifelsohne auch ein
Anliegen der psychedelischen Kunst und Kultur der 1960er
Jahre, die Dybbroe Møller ebenfalls als Referenz nennt.
Es ist eine Referenz, die sich vielleicht nicht auf
oberflächliche Ähnlichkeiten beschränkt, sondern darauf
hindeutet, dass in der Befreiung der Farbe, die Dybbroe
Møllers Arbeit vollzieht, eine psychedelische Methode
ihren Ausdruck findet. Fluoreszierende Farben und das
Lichtspektakel amorpher Kleckse psychedelischer Kunst und
Kultur waren eine eigensinnige, affektive Vulgarisierung
des Universalismus abstrakter Kunst. Nicht nur als

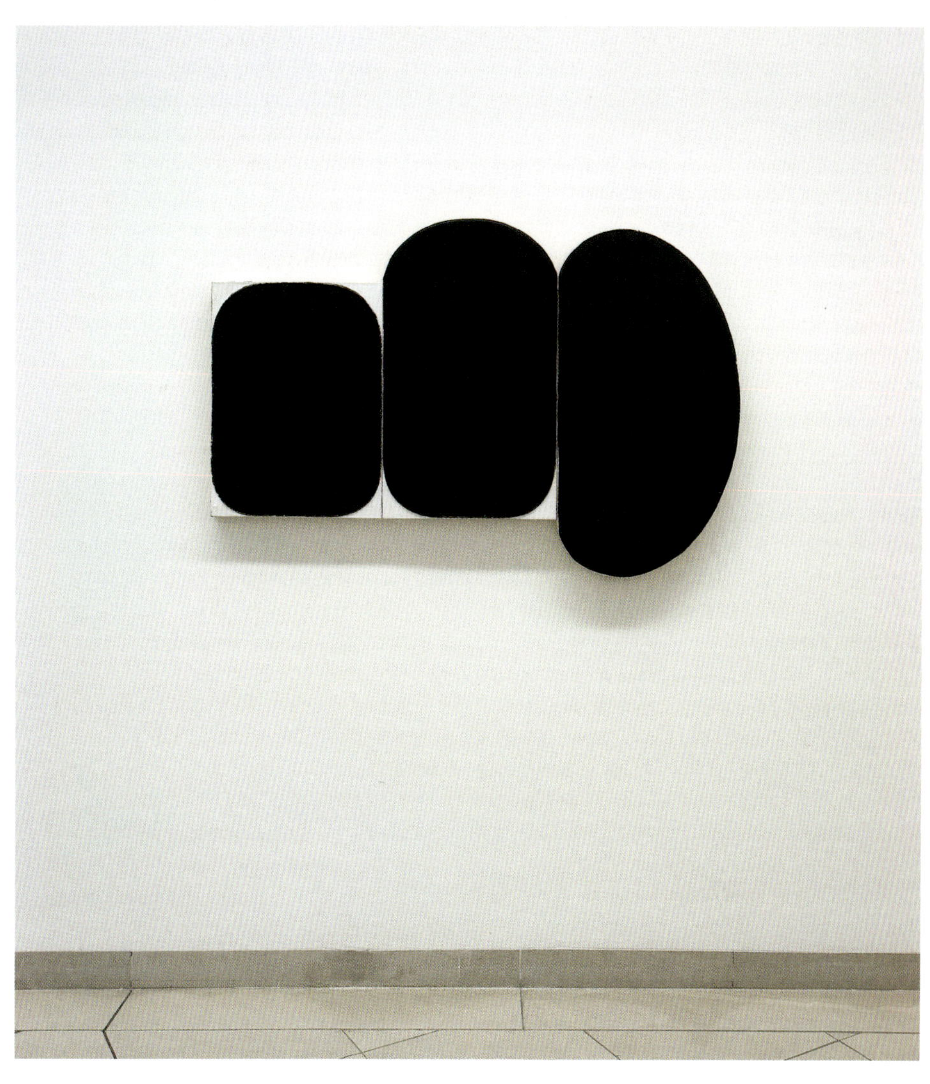

Gary Kuehn
<u>Black Painting</u>, 1972

referenzloses Spiel abstrakter Formen konnten sie gelesen werden, sondern durch die Dominanz der Farbe über die Form auch als Visualisierung des Blutstroms und seiner chemischen Transformationen. Farbe wurde von der Bildebene befreit und in eine konkrete, aber entkörperlichte Präsenz im sozialen Raum verwandelt: verführerisch und molekular, wie ein Geist oder Gas. Eine weitere für Dybbroe Møllers Arbeit relevante psychedelische Referenz ist die sog. ›Blotter Art‹, also die winzigen Motive, die Drogenunternehmer für die briefmarkengroßen, mit flüssigem LSD durchtränkten Löschpapiere entwerfen lassen, um unterschiedliche Trips oder ›Marken‹ identifizieren zu können. Wie wir sehen werden, bezieht sich Black, White and Gray (Cyan, Magenta and Yellow) auf minimalistische und konzeptuelle Kunst sowohl hinsichtlich ihrer Methode als auch des kunstgeschichtlichen Fakts. Doch der als Psychedelia bezeichnete Stil, der nicht kartographierte Energien wie einen kunsthistorischen Delinquenten mit barocken Neigungen in sich birgt, könnte gut die dritte Zutat sein, die Dybbroe Møllers Arbeit ihre besondere Dynamik verleiht. Die Verwendung von Farbe, die Beschwörung des Psychedelischen und dessen Mobilisierung von Affekt sind vor dem Hintergrund der Ausstellung Black, White and Gray besehen natürlich ironisch, sollte sie doch gerade einem Gegengewicht zum Action Painting und dessen »Empfindsamkeit der Farbe«, wie Wagstaff Jr. schrieb, Raum geben.[VI]

   Doch was ist dann die kunstgeschichtliche Erzählung, die Black, White and Gray (Cyan, Magenta and Yellow) aus den vielschichtigen Sedimenten herausschält und bricht? Donald Judds Besprechung von Black, White and Gray – er war in der Ausstellung selbst nicht vertreten – trug ebenso viel dazu bei wie die Ausstellung selbst, dass sie zu einem Meilenstein minimalistischer Kunst wurde. In seinem lakonischen Werturteil über die Ausstellung und die gezeigten Arbeiten formulierte Judd genau das, was zu

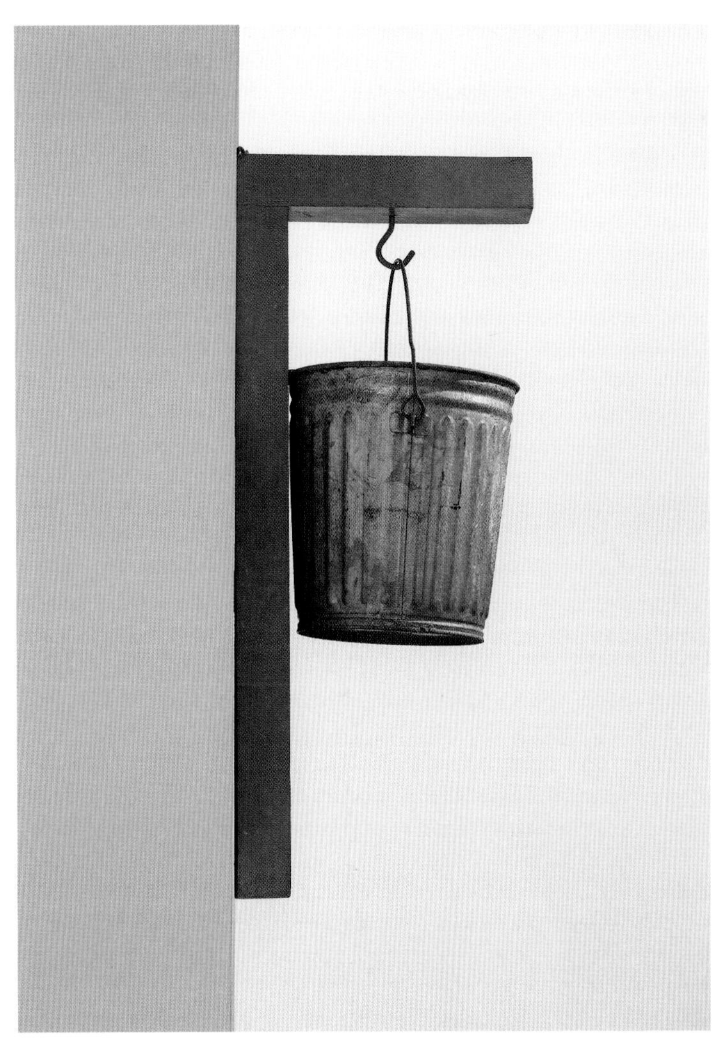

Robert Morris
Fountain, 1963

den Charakteristika der Minimal Art werden sollte. Eine
Kunst konstatierend, die »flache, nicht-wertende Sicht-
weisen« ausdrücke, schrieb er:

> Eine Arbeit ist ein vertrauter Gegenstand oder eine,
> oft ebenfalls vertraute, Abbildung eines solchen. Sie
> scheint nicht Kunst zu sein. Alles, was sie zu sein
> behauptet, ist, ausgestellt zu sein. Sie wird als
> Kunst gezeigt und wird dadurch Gegenständen gleich,
> die offenkundig Kunst sind. Die Wichtigkeit von Kunst
> wird auf alles ausgedehnt, und das meiste davon ist
> banal, gewöhnlich und unbeachtet. Man wird gezwungen,
> die gewöhnlichen Dinge zu beachten und alles zu hinter-
> fragen, was in der Kunst als wichtig gegolten hat.
> [...] Mit beliebig vielen neuen Objekten, Materialien
> und Techniken könnte Kunst gemacht werden.[VII]

Bei der zweiten Präsentation, diesmal im MMK in Frankfurt
am Main, bildete Black, White and Gray (Cyan, Magenta
and Yellow) die Bühne für eine Auswahl von Arbeiten aus
der Sammlung des Museums. Zwei davon waren auch in der
Ausstellung von 1964 gewesen: Jim Dines Black Bathroom #1
(1962) und Andy Warhols White Disaster II (1963).[VIII] Die von
MMK Direktor Udo Kittelmann kombinierten Arbeiten brachten
Künstler der ursprünglichen Konstellation mit anderen
kanonischen Nordamerikanern zusammen, deren künstlerische
Praxis sich als minimalistisch, geometrisch und nicht-
kompositorisch charakterisieren lässt: Neben Dine und
Warhol waren dies Jo Baer, Donald Judd, Gary Kuehn, Walter
De Maria, Bruce Nauman, Robert Morris, Robert Ryman und
Cy Twombly. Vor dem Hintergrund von Black, White and Gray
(Cyan, Magenta and Yellow) kehrten diese Arbeiten in der
MMK-Ausstellung aus dem Archiv ins Leben zurück - sowohl
historisch als auch physisch, jedoch auf zwei Dimensionen
reduziert -, als wären sie aus dem Bild genommen und ihre
unmittelbare Präsenz dadurch um 43 Jahre verzögert worden.

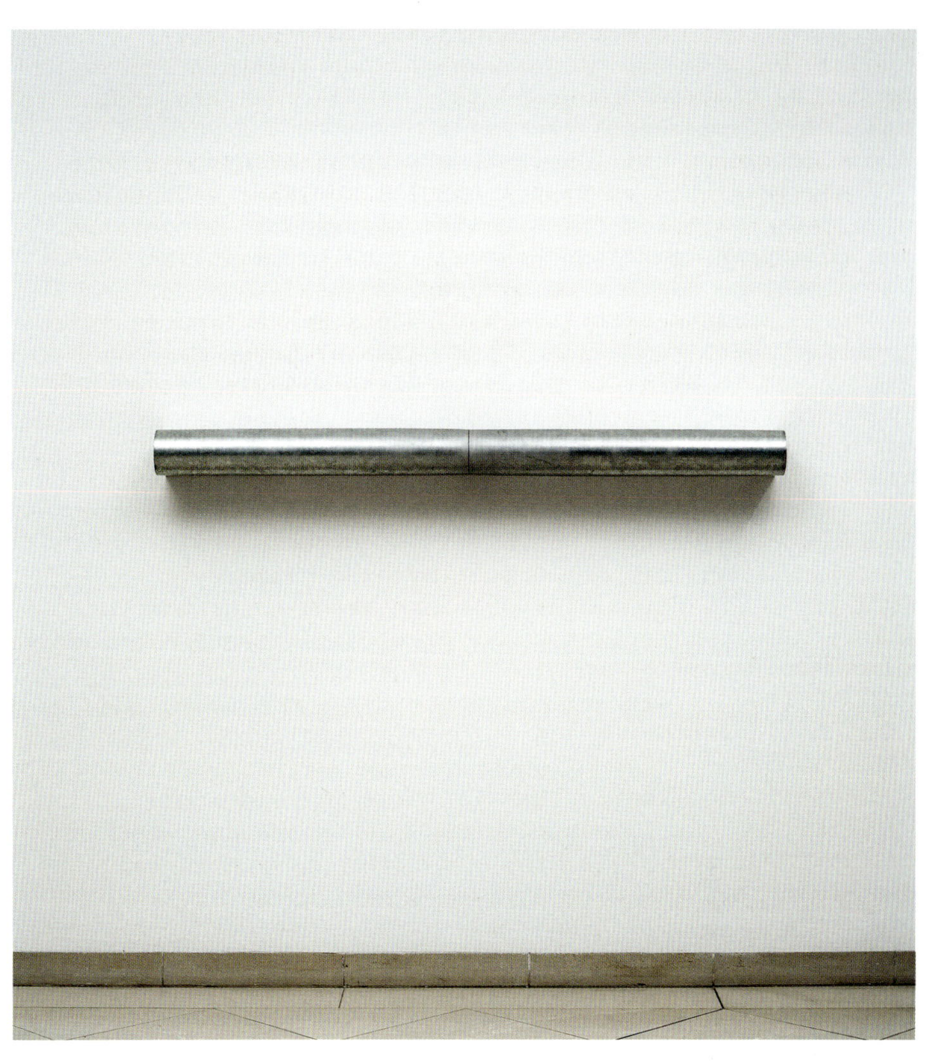

Donald Judd
Untitled (#94, 1967), 1988

Nur wenige der im MMK ausgewählten Arbeiten repräsentieren kompromisslosen Minimalismus: Wohl nur in Bezug auf Walter De Marias glatten und engen Cage (1965), die drei Arbeiten von Judd (zwei ›Regal‹-Arbeiten und eine Bodenarbeit aus einer schwarzen keilförmigen Metallplatte) und die Arbeit der einzigen Frau in dieser Auswahl, Jo Baer (mit einem Diptychon aus monochromen weißen Leinwänden, eingefasst von schwarzen, gemalten Rahmen – eine buchstäbliche Hard-Edge-Arbeit), kann davon die Rede sein. Einige der anderen Arbeiten bringen narrative und reduzierende Impulse auf Kollisionskurs zueinander, zum Beispiel Bruce Naumans Video From Flesh to White to Black to Flesh (1968), in dem der Künstler weißes und schwarzes Pigment auf seinen Körper aufträgt und wieder entfernt, oder Robert Morris' Fountain (1963): Aus einem hängenden verzinkten Eimer ertönt nicht das Geräusch seiner eigenen Herstellung, sondern das von laufendem Wasser. Ein Wortspiel mit Duchamp, kein Zweifel, im Zusammenhang mit der Arbeit Dybbroe Møllers, aber auch eines mit dem manieristischen Brunnen auf dem Foto. Andere Arbeiten stellen quasi-piktorialistische Albernheit in den Vordergrund, so wie Gary Kuehns Practitioner's Delight (1966): ein weißes Rechteck auf dem Boden, das scheinbar auf einer Seite aufgeschnitten wurde, wodurch seine ›Füllung‹ – eine leuchtend pinke Pfütze aus Plastik – herausfließen konnte. Minimalismus zum einfachen Verzehr, der mit dem ungebetenen Pink korrespondiert, das in Dybbroe Møllers Arbeit an den mit Tapetenkleister getränkten Stellen hervortritt. Robert Ryman schließlich steuert mit Adelphi (1967) die etwas schäbige Materialität eines weißen Monochroms bei.

Die Arbeiten in der Installationsansicht aus dem Atheneum sind offensichtlich auf zwei Dimensionen reduziert. Doch diese dimensionale Reduktion, die Black, White and Gray (Cyan, Magenta and Yellow) vollzieht, ist nur Schein. Durch eine Reihe widersprüchlicher Schachzüge wird die Arbeit zur Erforschung eines kunsthistorischen

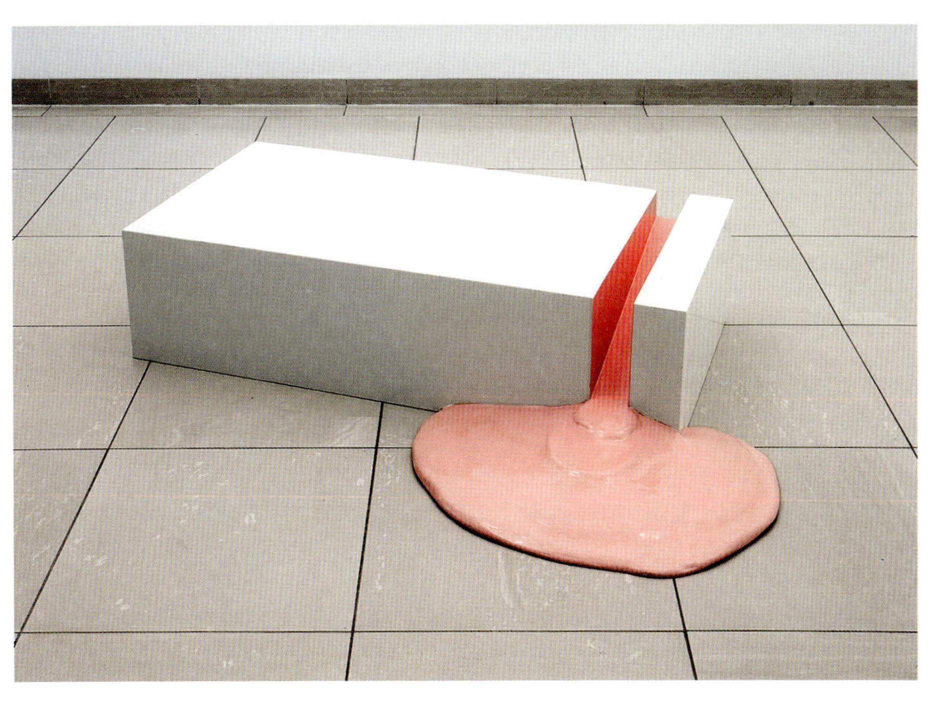

Gary Kuehn
<u>Practitioner's Delight</u>, 1966

Dokuments mit mehrschichtiger Dynamik. Ein Ausdruck dieser Dynamik ist beispielsweise das Gefecht zwischen Malerei und Skulptur; immer ein umkämpftes Gebiet jener ambitionierten Kunst des Modernismus, die sich mit dem Schaffen von Raum beschäftigte. (Insofern alle Arbeiten in der Ausstellung diesen beiden Kategorien angehörten, behandelte auch Black, White and Gray, wenngleich implizit, dieses Thema.) In Dybbroe Møllers Arbeit ist der abgebildete Raum nicht nur einmal repräsentiert (nämlich fotografisch), sondern zweimal, da er in Lebensgröße bzw. ü b e r l e b e n s g r o ß erscheint. Dybbroe Møller bleibt dem Minimalismus treu, indem er in einem Raster arbeitet und Materialien verwendet, denen dieser Bedeutung zusprach. Doch genau hierin liegt die Ironie, denn das bedeutungsvolle Material ist just die schwarze Tinte, aus der heraus sich gerade jene Farben entfalten, die die Ausstellung Black, White and Gray im Sinne einer Reduzierung des visuellen Ereignisses unterdrückte. Diese vielschichtige Neuauflage des minimalistischen Erbes macht Black, White and Gray (Cyan, Magenta and Yellow) so bombastisch wie einen Anselm Kiefer und so fragil wie einen Gustaf Metzger.

Hiermit verweist Dybbroe Møllers Arbeit auf die Spannungsfelder innerhalb des Minimalismus selbst: Sein transzendentaler Anspruch der ›flachen, nichtwertenden‹ Sichtweise, steht in Opposition zum Insistieren auf A t t i t ü d e , welche wiederum Interesse oder Intention voraussetzt (Judd und Wagstaff evozieren beide die neue ›Attitüde‹ in ihren Besprechungen von Black, White and Gray). Zugleich fordert Dybbroe Møllers Arbeit aber auch die Kritiker des Minimalismus heraus, darunter Michael Fried als den angesehensten. Frieds spätmodernistische Betonung der ›Optikalität‹ als Voraussetzung für die körperlose Erfahrung des vollkommen präsenten Kunst-objekts erhält in Black, White and Gray (Cyan, Magenta and Yellow) eine paradoxe Wendung, da es eben die der

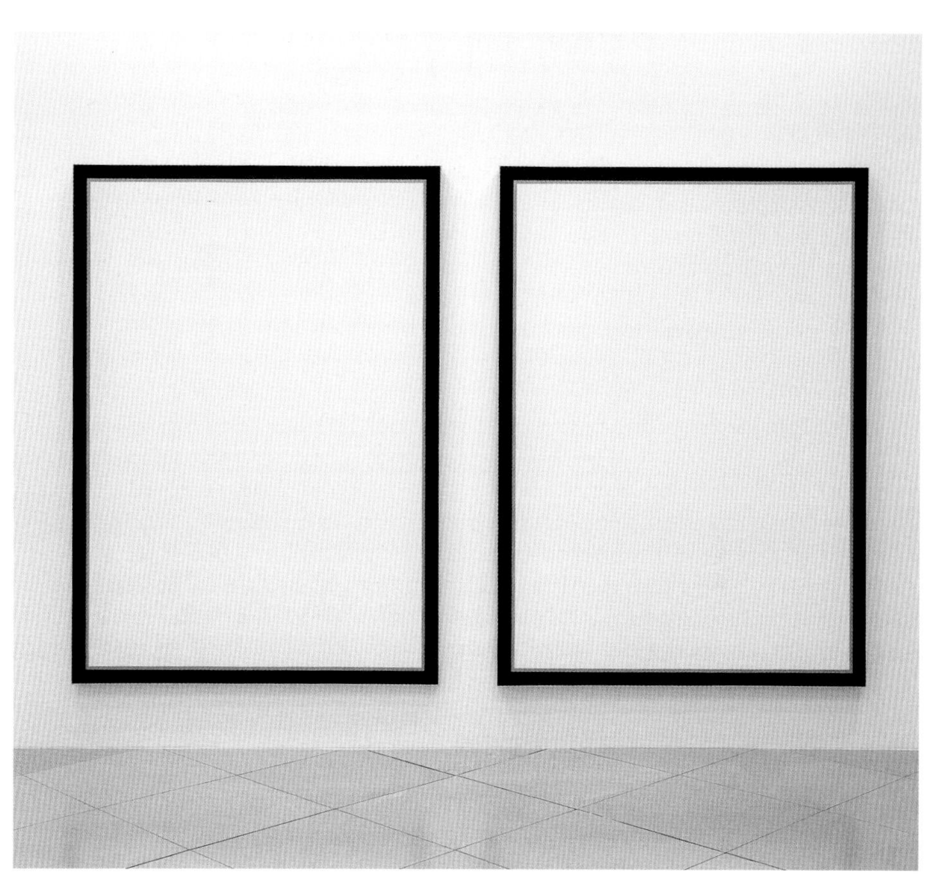

Jo Baer
<u>Ohne Titel (Diptych)</u>, 1966-70

Arbeit eigene Optikalität ist, ihre seltsame Visualität,
die sie zu einer so viszeralen Arbeit macht - vielleicht
mehr als ihre Größe: Die sichtbare Korrosion des Bildes
verwandelt es in ein Lebewesen. Auf diese Weise wird die
kunsthistorische Vertäuung des Minimalismus und seiner
Kritik gelöst und in der Gegenwart wieder flott gemacht.
So verleiht Dybbroe Møller einer historischen Kunstform
wieder Kraft, indem er in die disziplinäre Infrastruktur
interveniert, mittels welcher ihre Geschichte geschrieben
wurde: das Museum und seine archivierenden Methoden.

3.
Während andere Arbeiten von Dybbroe Møller fotografisch
sind, bedient sich <u>Black, White and Gray (Cyan, Magenta
and Yellow)</u> der Fotografie vielmehr als temporäres
Instrument in einer spezifischen Art und Weise. Indem
die schwarzen und weißen Ausdrucke mittels Kleister
›entwickelt‹ werden, entsteht ein seltsames Nachbild des
ursprünglichen Fotos. Dies hängt mit der Herstellungsweise
der Arbeit zusammen: das Ausdrucken entspricht im Grunde
dem Kopieren, also einer ebenfalls fotografischen Technik,
die darüber hinaus auf P r o j e k t i o n basiert - mit
allem was dies für eine zukünftige Nutzung impliziert.
Sie ermöglicht Reproduktionen, die dem Modell exakt
entsprechen. Am Ende der 1960er Jahre war eine billigere,
schnellere und demokratischere Produktionsweise in der
Kunst nicht vorstellbar. Marshall McLuhan schrieb 1967:

> Die Xerographie - geistiger Diebstahl für alle -
> kündigt die Zeiten des Sofortbuches an. Jedermann
> kann nun Autor und Verleger zugleich werden. Man
> nehme beliebige Bücher über ein beliebiges Thema
> und stelle sich dann mittels einer einfachen
> Vervielfältigung des Kapitels von diesem, eines
> andern von jenem Buch sein eigenes maßgeschneidertes
> Buch her - das Sofortplagiat![IX]

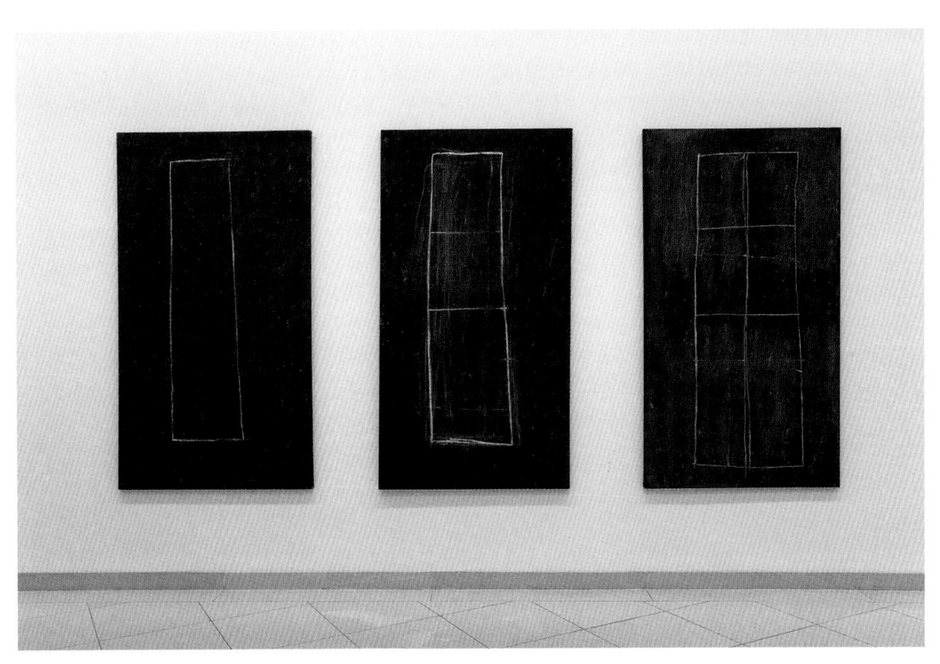

Cy Twombly

<u>Problem I, II, III</u>, 1966

Heute sind Kopieren und Drucken natürlich banale Repro-
duktionstechniken (was McLuhan etwas aufregender als
›stehlen‹ bezeichnete). Im Kontext von Black, White and
Gray (Cyan, Magenta and Yellow) führen diese Techniken
zu einer Vorgehensweise, die mit ihrem einfachen und
reduzierten Anti-Formalismus dem Konzeptualismus
näher steht als dem Anliegen der ›Repräsentation als
Realisierung‹ im Minimalismus. Dies erinnert daran, dass
die erste Generation der New Yorker Konzeptualisten
behauptete, die minimalistischen Künstler hätten ihr
eigenes Prinzip der Trennung von Material und Idee nicht
zu einer logischen Konsequenz geführt.

Das herkömmliche Misstrauen gegenüber der Fotografie
als Kunst basiert darauf, dass sie kein Original hervor-
bringe, sondern immer eine (Foto)Kopie sei. Eine weitere,
ernstere Realität des fotografischen Bildes ist die der
festgehaltenen Zeit, aus der die Toten zu uns zurück-
schauen, wie Roland Barthes es formulierte. Im Foto vom
Wadsworth Atheneum sind es nicht nur die minimalistischen
Arbeiten, die zu uns zurückblicken, sondern auch
Francavillas Venus: ein mythologisches weibliches Wesen,
das uns vom Manierismus aus durch die Jahrhunderte
hindurch betrachtet – also aus der Perspektive jener
Epoche, in der sich die Kunst zum ersten Mal ihrer selbst
bewusst wurde. In ihrer Opulenz kontrastiert die Skulptur
den Look eleganter Verweigerung, der den um die Mitte des
20. Jahrhunderts entstandenen Arbeiten zu Eigen ist, die
den Brunnen auf dem Foto umgeben.

Dybbroe Møllers Arbeit liefert ein genauso visuell
rätselhaftes wie physisch einnehmendes Bild: zusammengesetzt aus zwei Originalen, vergrößert, in kleine Teile
zerschnitten und korrodiert; die zweischneidige Zeitlich-
keit einer Szene, die so tief ist wie 400 Jahre Kunst-
geschichte und so flach wie eine Fotokopie, auf sich
selbst zurückgeworfen und mit künstlicher Patina über-
zogen. Man sagt, dass Hellseher die Toten nicht als blasse

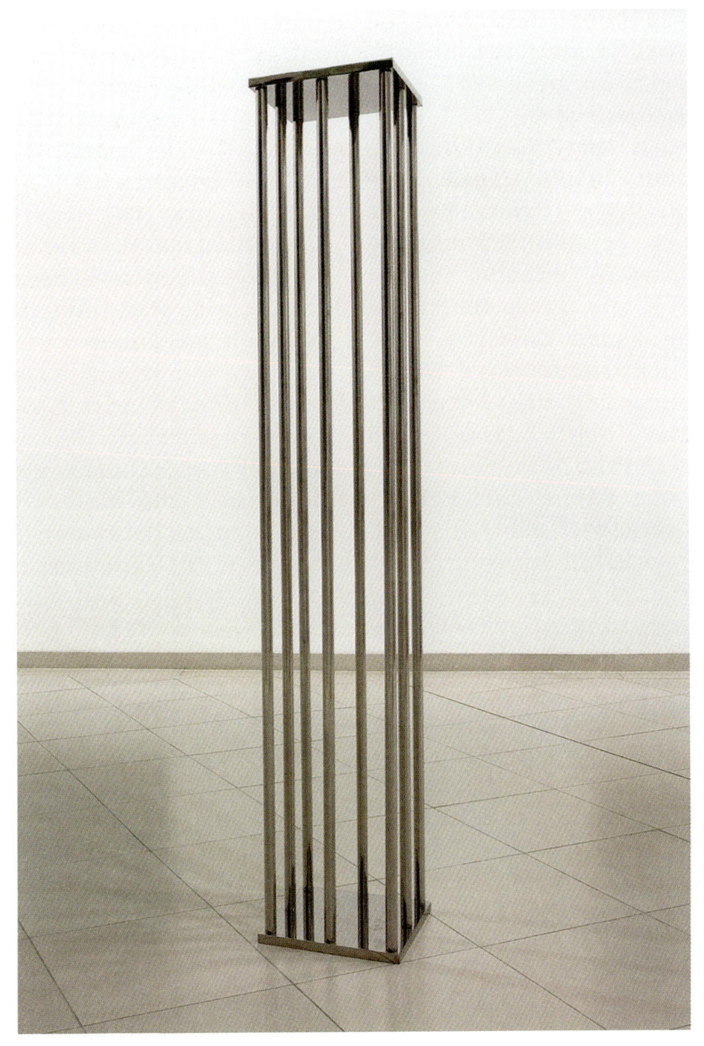

Walter De Maria
<u>Cage</u>, 1965

Geister, sondern als farbige Punkte oder verschwommene
Abwesenheiten im Raum sehen. Wenn wir beginnen uns
in der Zeit zu bewegen, könnten wir vielleicht etwas
Ähnlichem begegnen, wie wenn wir uns in andere räumliche
Dimensionen begeben: kontinuierliches Grau oder kräftige,
leuchtende Farben wie H.G. Wells sie beschreibt. <u>Black,
White and Gray (Cyan, Magenta and Yellow)</u> ist das Bild
eines verblichenen Pantheons, das verbraucht aussieht
und unwiederbringlich ins Archiv abgestiegen scheint, das
uns jedoch wie eine blutende Heiligendarstellung durch
sickernde Farbe beweist, dass es noch am Leben ist. Aber
sein ›Bluten‹ ist eher profan als transzendental; es ist
der Effekt, der das Foto aus dem transhistorischen Raum
zurück ins Jetzt bringt.

    Vielleicht versinnbildlicht Dybbroe Møllers Ver-
wendung von Farbe letztlich zwei Dinge: zum einen die
Tendenz jeder (kunst)historischen Kategorisierung,
künstlerische Phänomene in Narrationen zu bündeln, die
die Kunst spezifizieren, die sie zum Gegenstand haben.
Diese Bündelung geschieht immer mit dem Risiko, Arbeiten
auszuschließen, die eigentlich relevant sind, aber nicht
›passen‹. Ein explizites Beispiel einer erzwungenen
Narration ist die Art und Weise, wie Wagstaff Warhol davon
zu überzeugen versuchte, eine Gruppe weißer <u>Brillo</u>-Boxen
für die Ausstellung <u>Black, White and Gray</u> zu produzieren,
da die Blau- und Rottöne der originalen <u>Brillo</u>-Boxen nicht
in das Konzept passten. Der Kunsthistoriker James Meyer
bemerkt dazu trocken, dass »Warhol stattdessen schließlich
zwei <u>White Disasters</u> schickte«.[x] Und wer hat jemals von
der <u>Pizza</u> aus Zement und der Skulptur <u>Dog Turd</u> gehört,
die Carl Andre in den frühen 1960er Jahren produzierte?
Warum haben wir darüber nie gelesen? Pizzen und Hunde-
haufen – unbestritten flache, nicht hierarchische,
nichtwertende Kunstwerke, die aber aus Bequemlichkeit
nichtsdestotrotz aus den meisten Darstellungen der Minimal
Art ausgefiltert wurden.

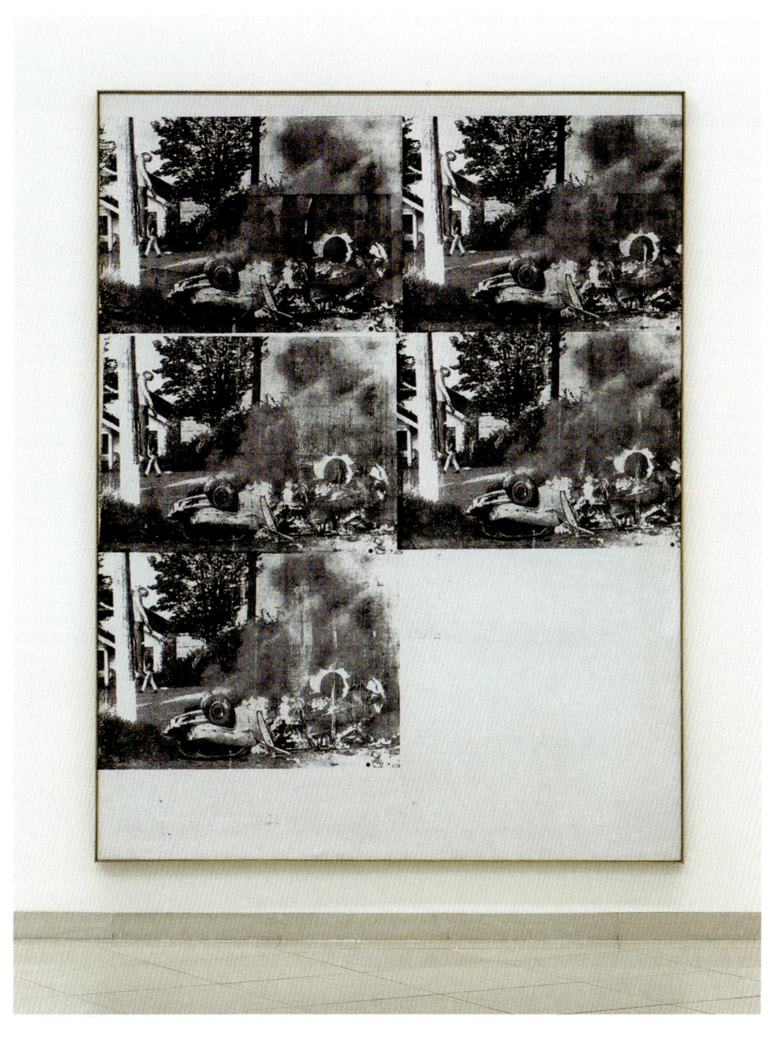

Andy Warhol
White Disaster II (White Burning Car II), 1963

Die Farbe in <u>Black, White and Gray (Cyan, Magenta and Yellow)</u> versinnbildlicht zum anderen aber auch die Art und Weise, wie die Rezeption einer Arbeit oder einer Ausstellung immer über die künstlerische Intention und Diskussion hinausgeht, und wie infolgedessen Kunst und der sie umgebende soziale Raum auf unerwartete Weise aufeinander abfärben. Laut dem stilbewussten Samuel Wagstaff Jr. wurde dies im Fall von <u>Black, White and Gray</u> daran deutlich, dass die Ausstellung bei der Redaktion der <u>Vogue</u> ein »wahnsinniger Erfolg« war und eine sechsseitige Fotostrecke erhielt. Unter dem Titel <u>Der letzte Schrei: die Begeisterung für Schwarzweiß ist zurück</u> brachte das Magazin unter anderem ein Foto von einem schwanenhalsigen Model mit die Schwerkraft überwindender Coiffure, das, posierend vor Morris' Arbeiten <u>Untitled (Column)</u> und <u>Untitled (Slab)</u>, ein Kleid in... Pink trug.[XI]

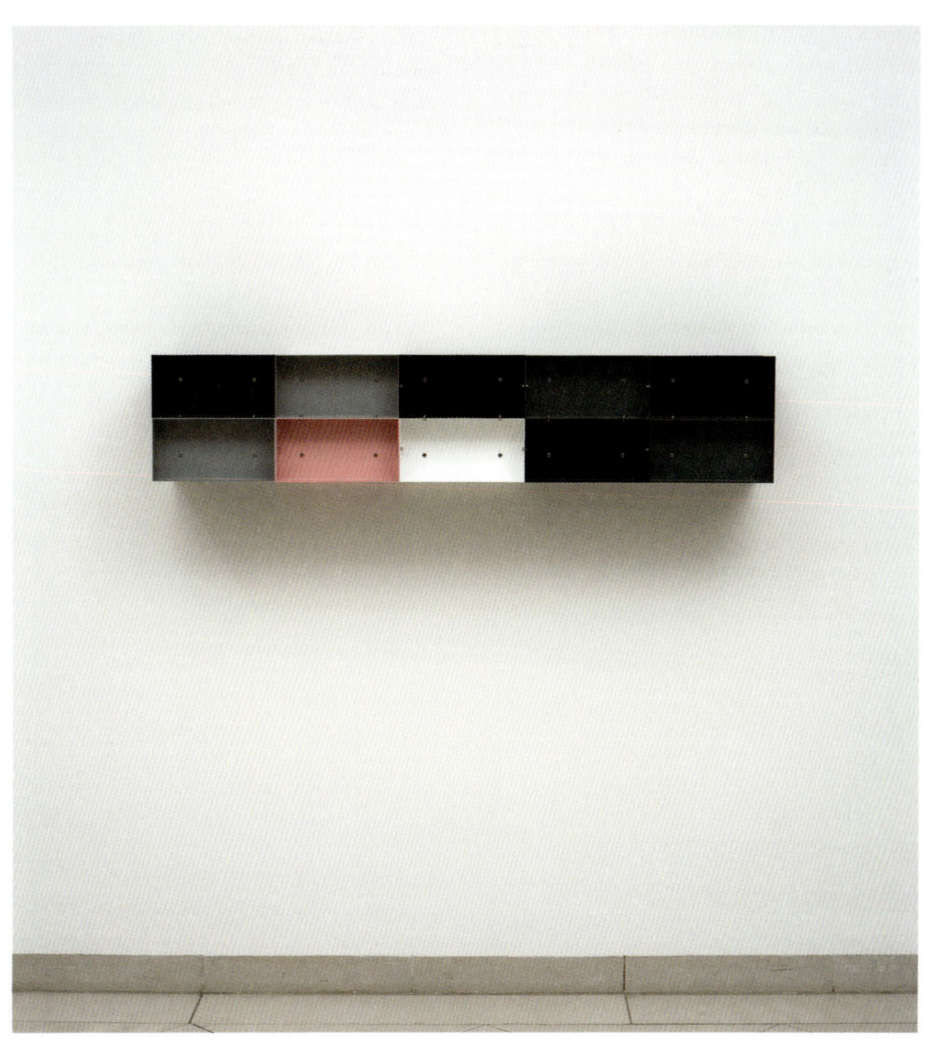

Donald Judd
<u>Untitled</u>, 1987

^I Donald Judd, »Schwarz, Weiß und Grau«, in: Gregor Stemmrich (Hg.), Minimal Art. Eine kritische Retrospektive, Dresden und Basel: Verlag der Kunst, 1995, S. 195-201, 195.

^{II} Vgl. James Meyers Beschreibung der Ausstellung in Minimalism. Art and Polemics in the Sixties, New Haven: Yale University Press, 2004 (2001), S. 76-81.

^{III} Simon Dybbroe Møller in einer E-Mail an den Autor, 3. Juli 2008.

^{IV} Herbert G. Wells, Die Zeitmaschine, Gütersloh: Bertelsmann Lesering, 1961, S. 36 f.

^V Vgl. Frederic Jameson, Archaeologies of the Future, London: Verso, 2005.

^{VI} Vgl. Meyer, S. 77.

^{VII} Judd, S. 199-200.

^{VIII} Über Warhol sagte Judd in seiner Rezension eher liebevoll, dass er »im Grunde ein Expressionist« sei (vgl. Judd, S. 200), eine Zuschreibung, die Warhol ermutigt haben muss, sein berufliches Profil dem anzupassen.

^{IX} Marshall McLuhan und Quentin Fiore, Das Medium ist Massage, Frankfurt am Main: Ullstein, 1969, S. 123.

^X Meyer, S. 78.

^{XI} Ebd.

Robert Ryman
<u>Adelphi</u>, 1967

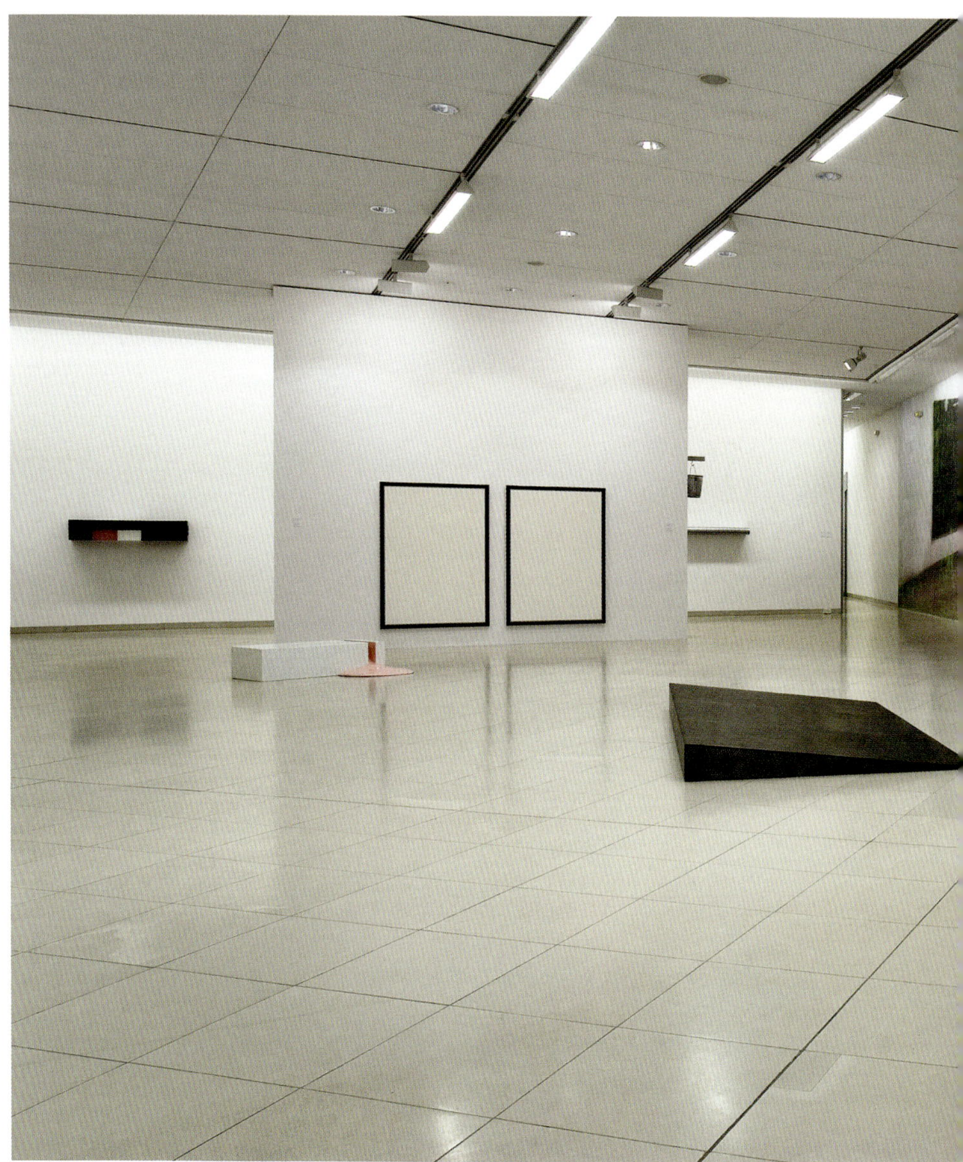

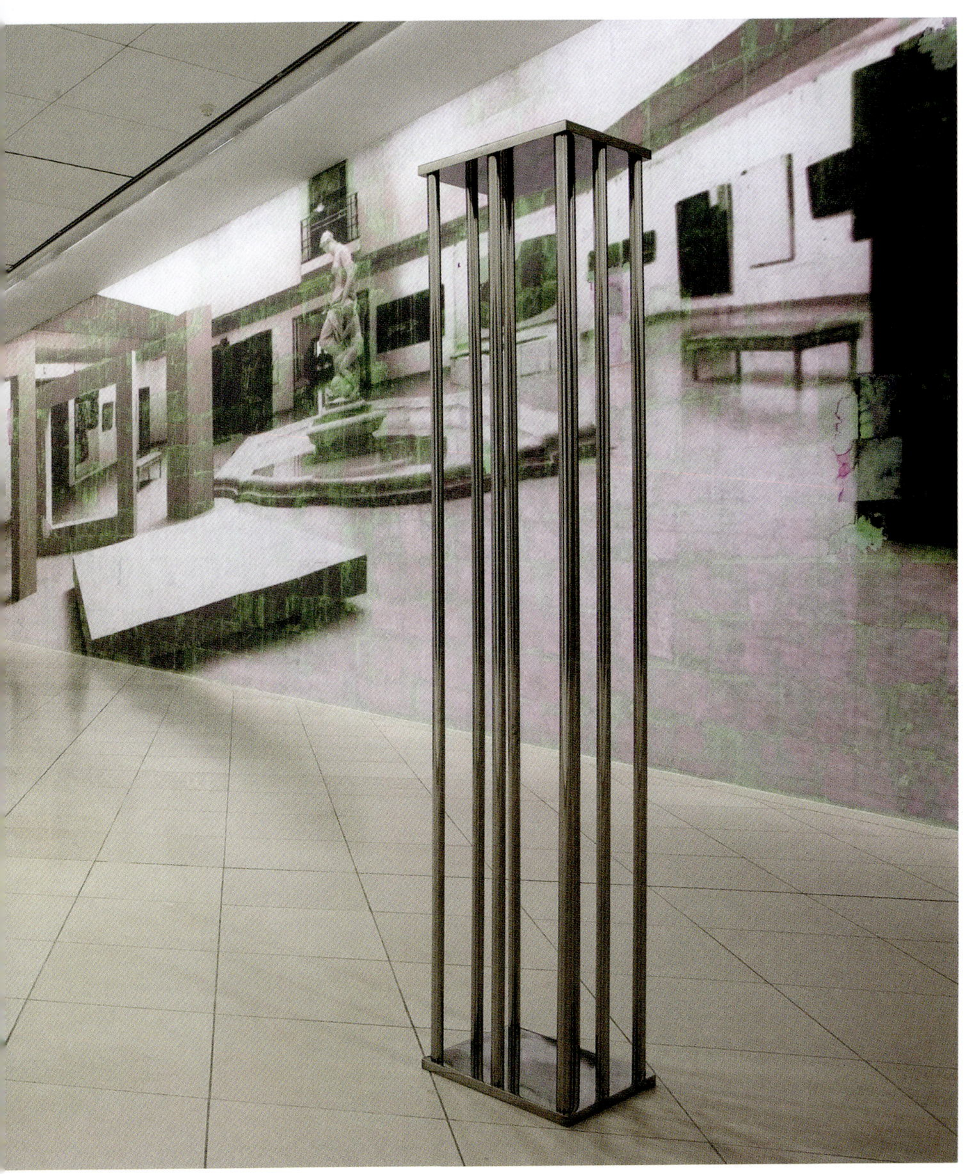

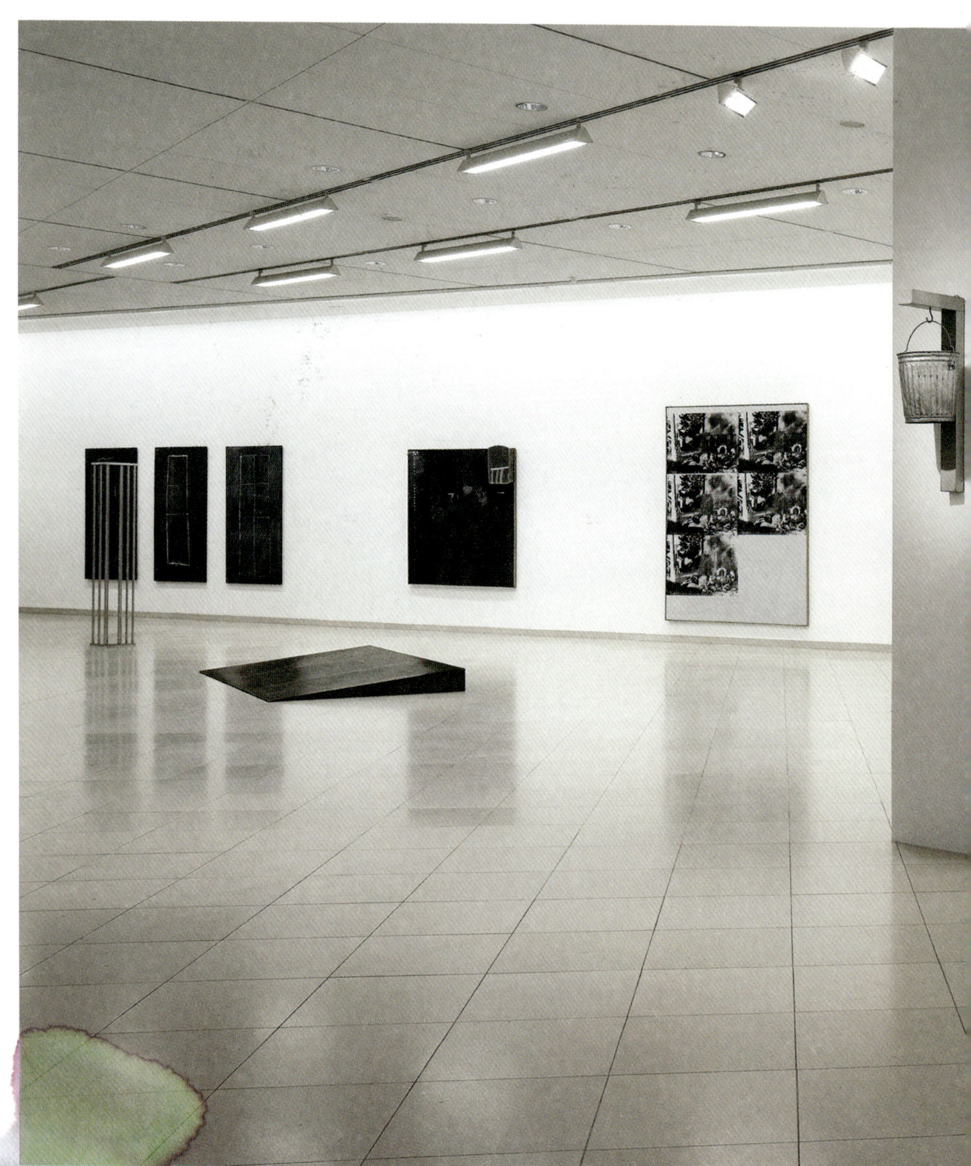

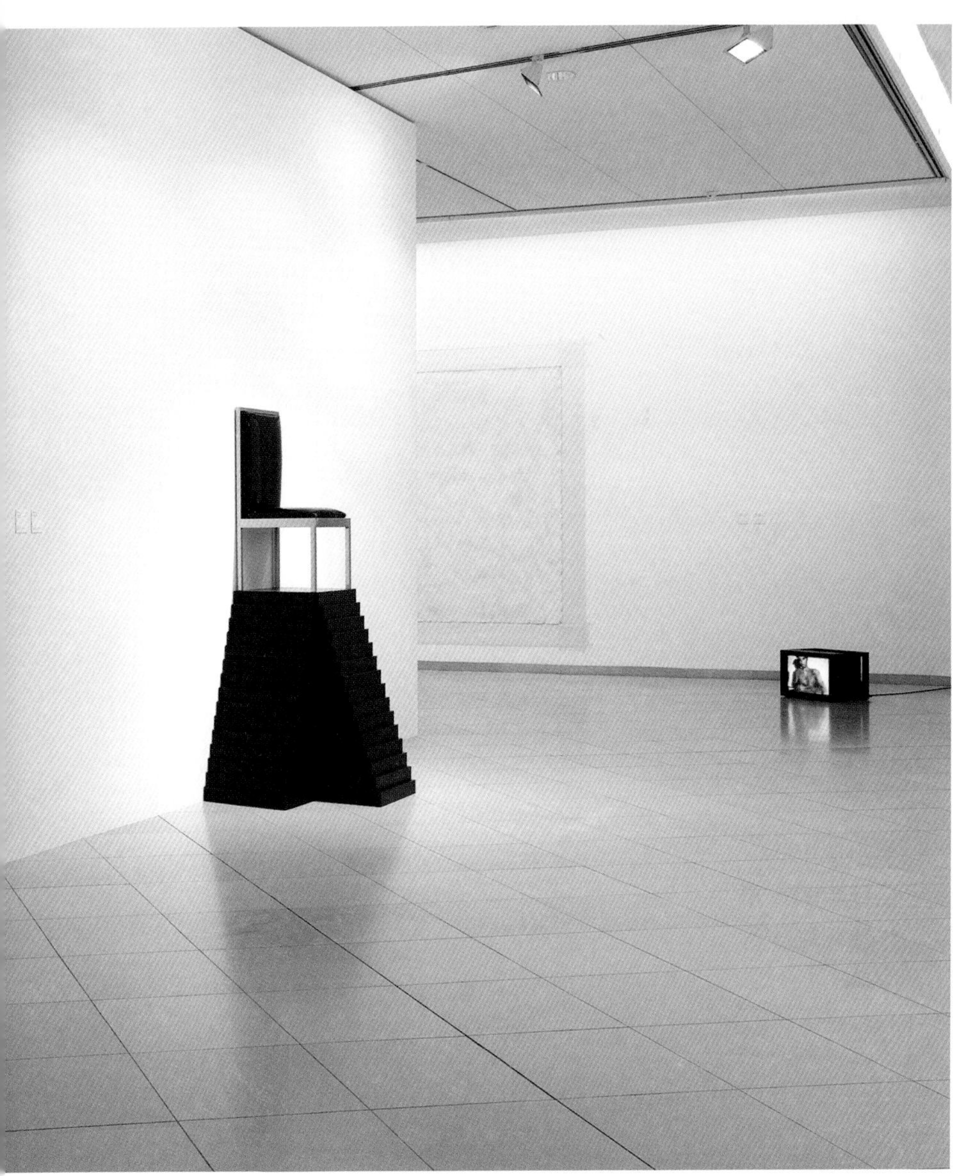

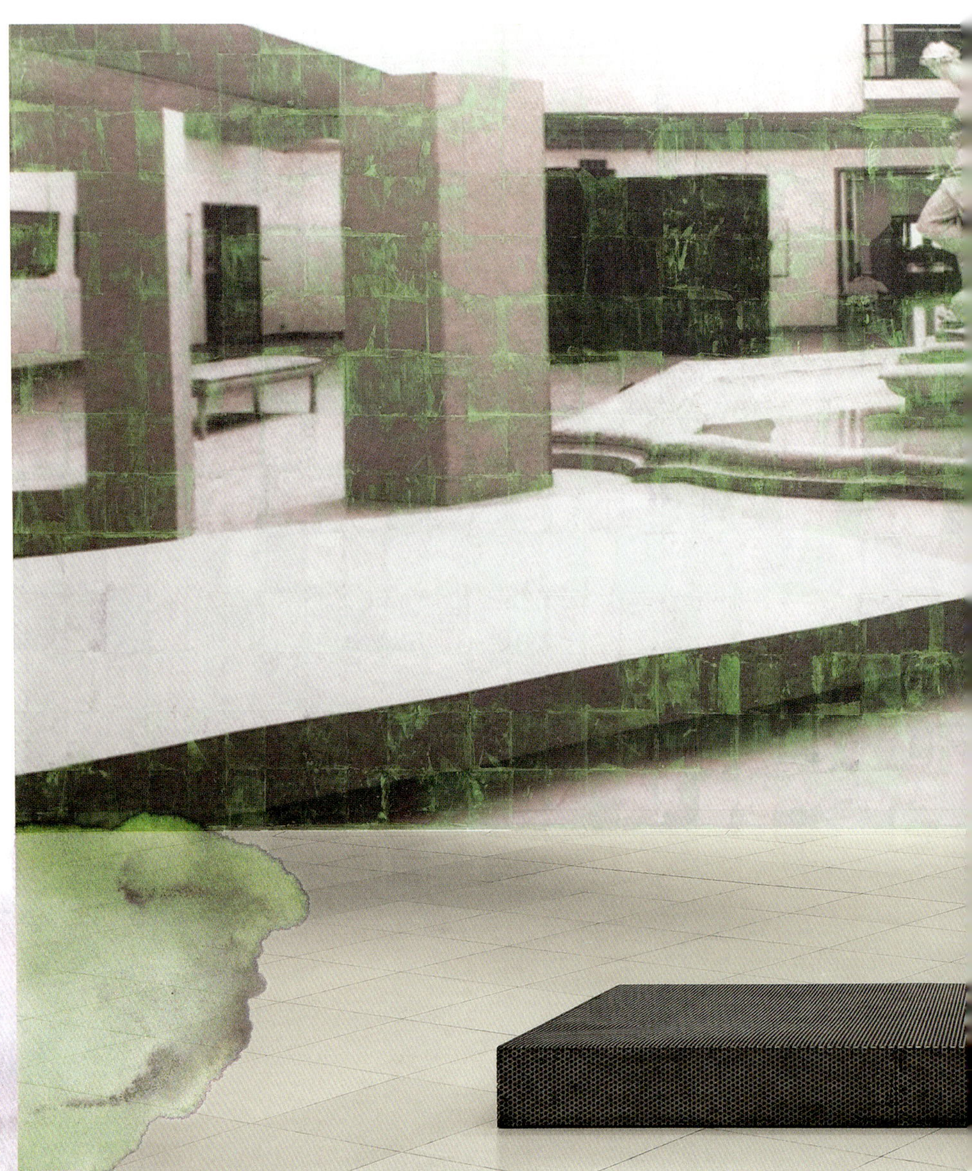

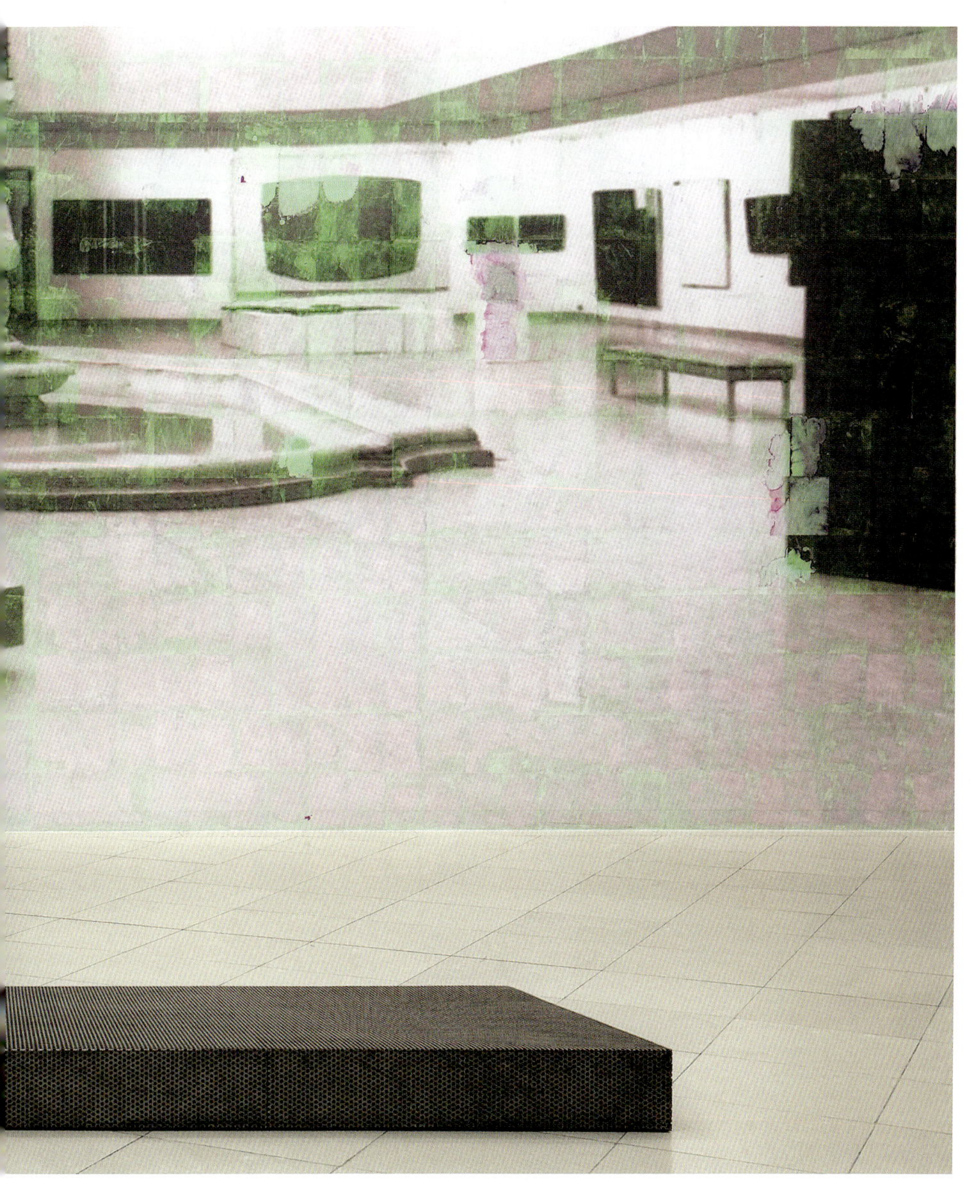

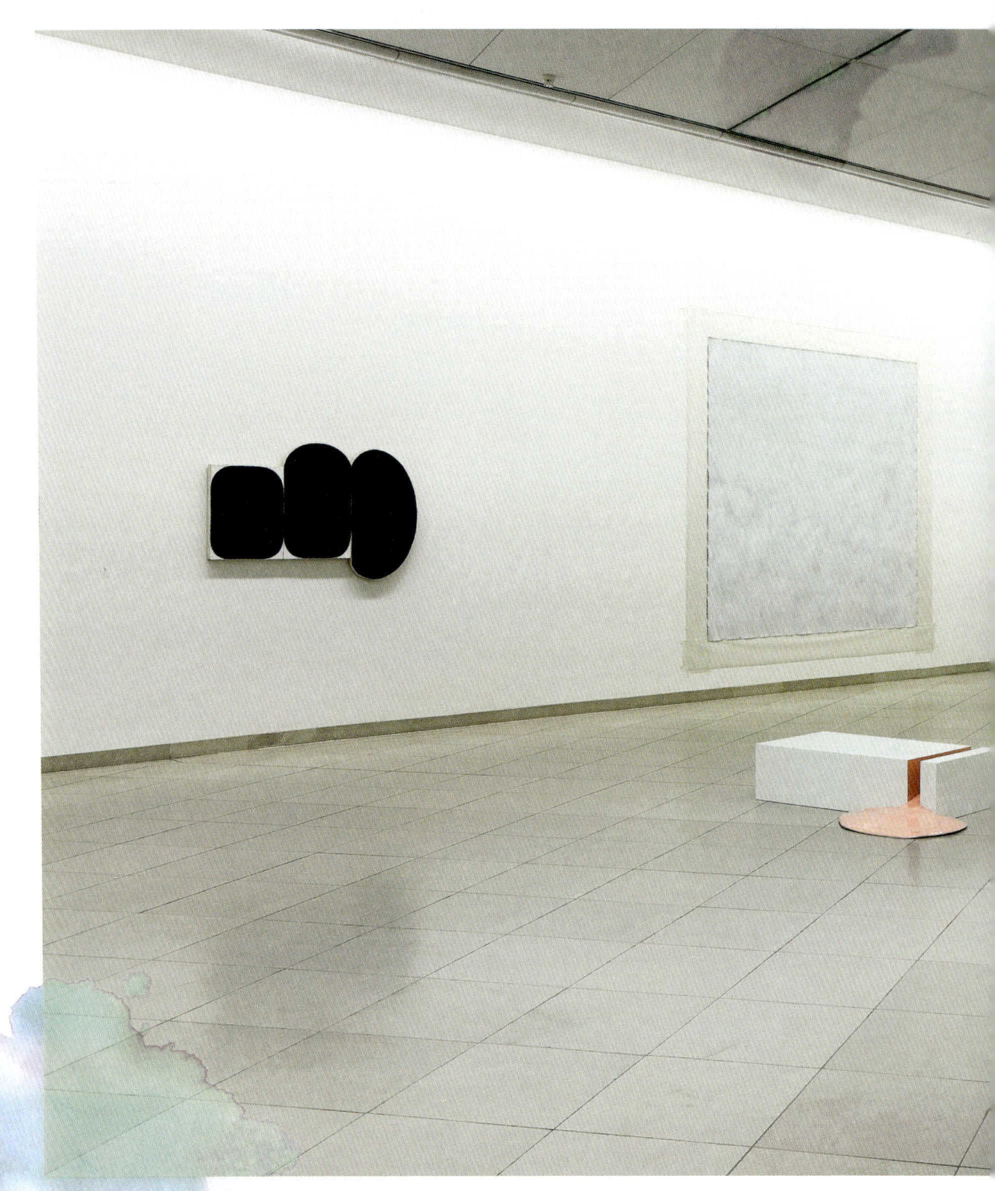

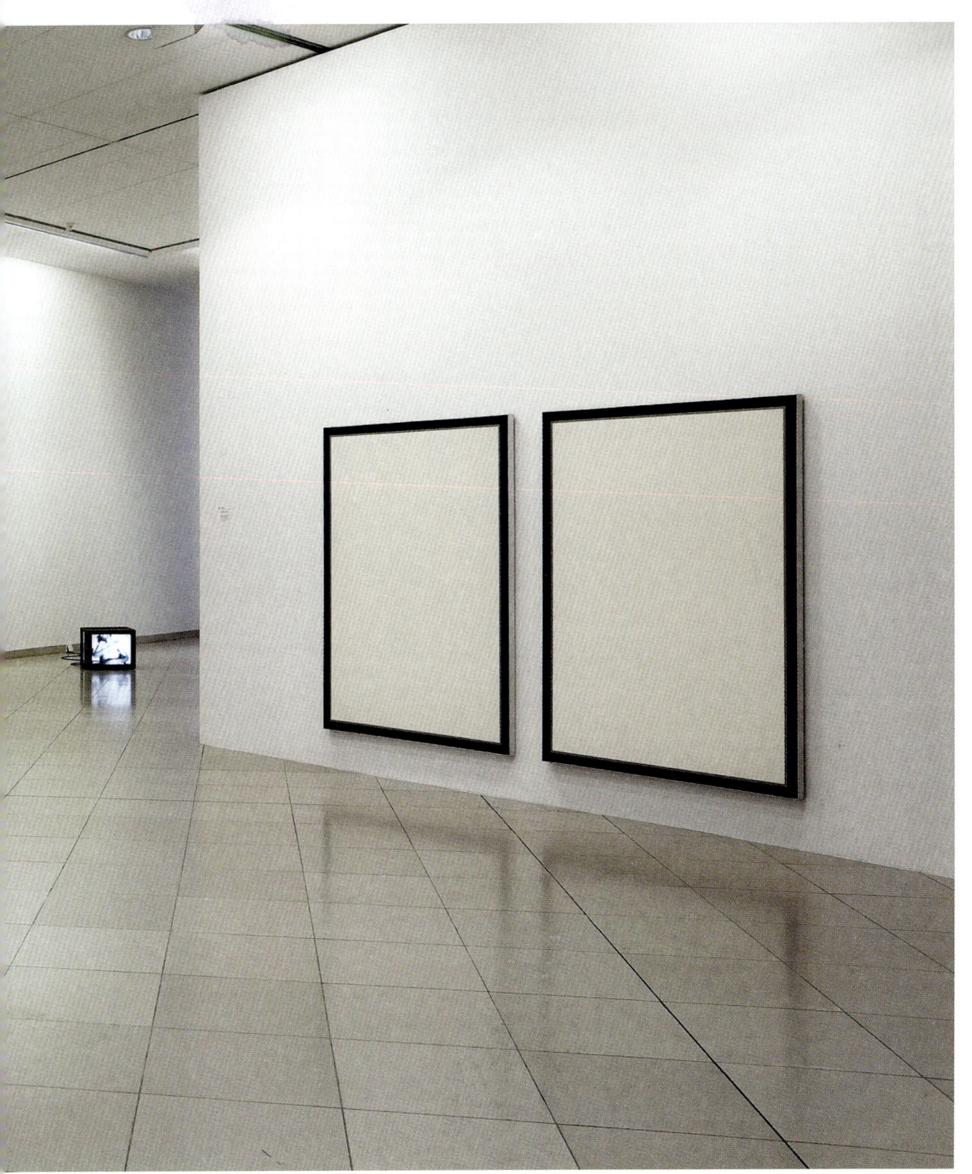

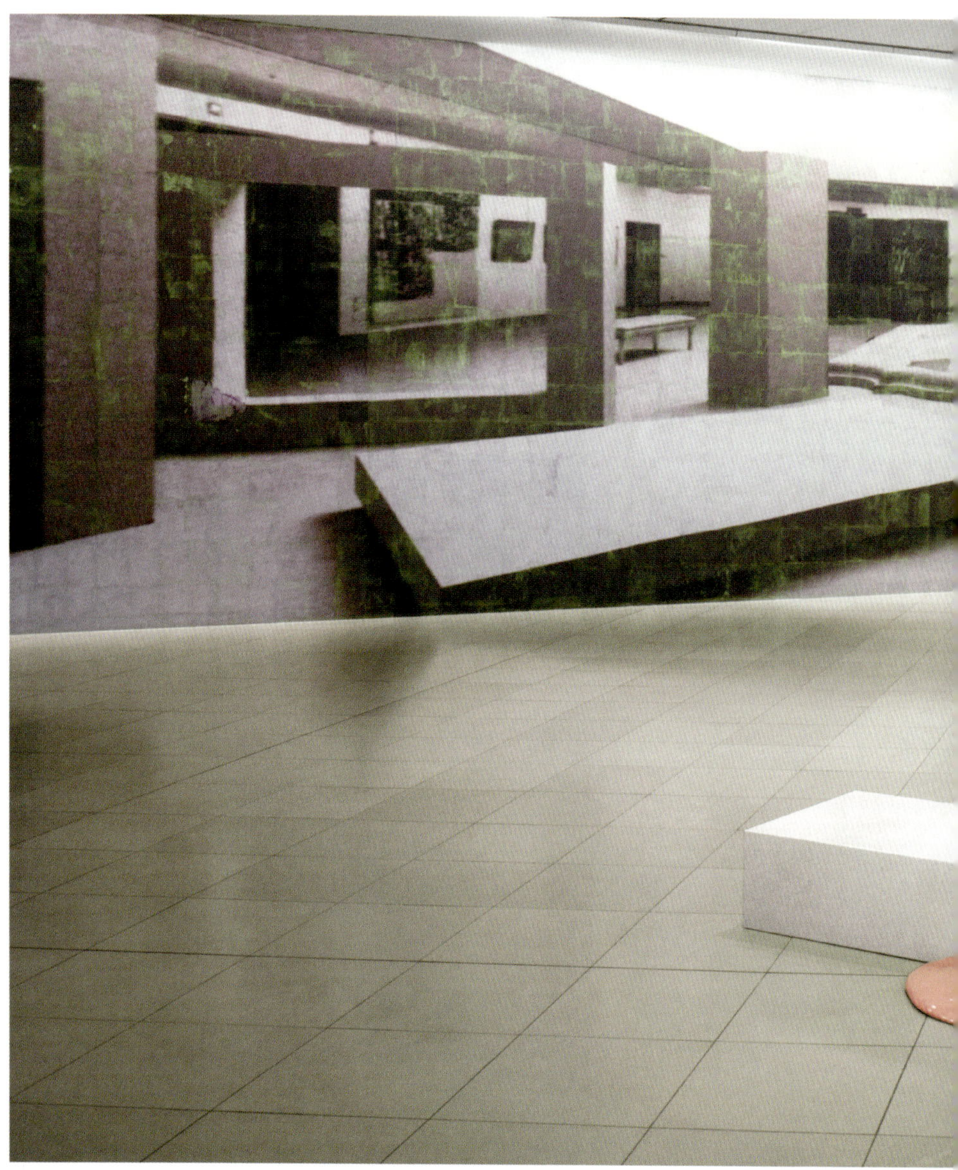

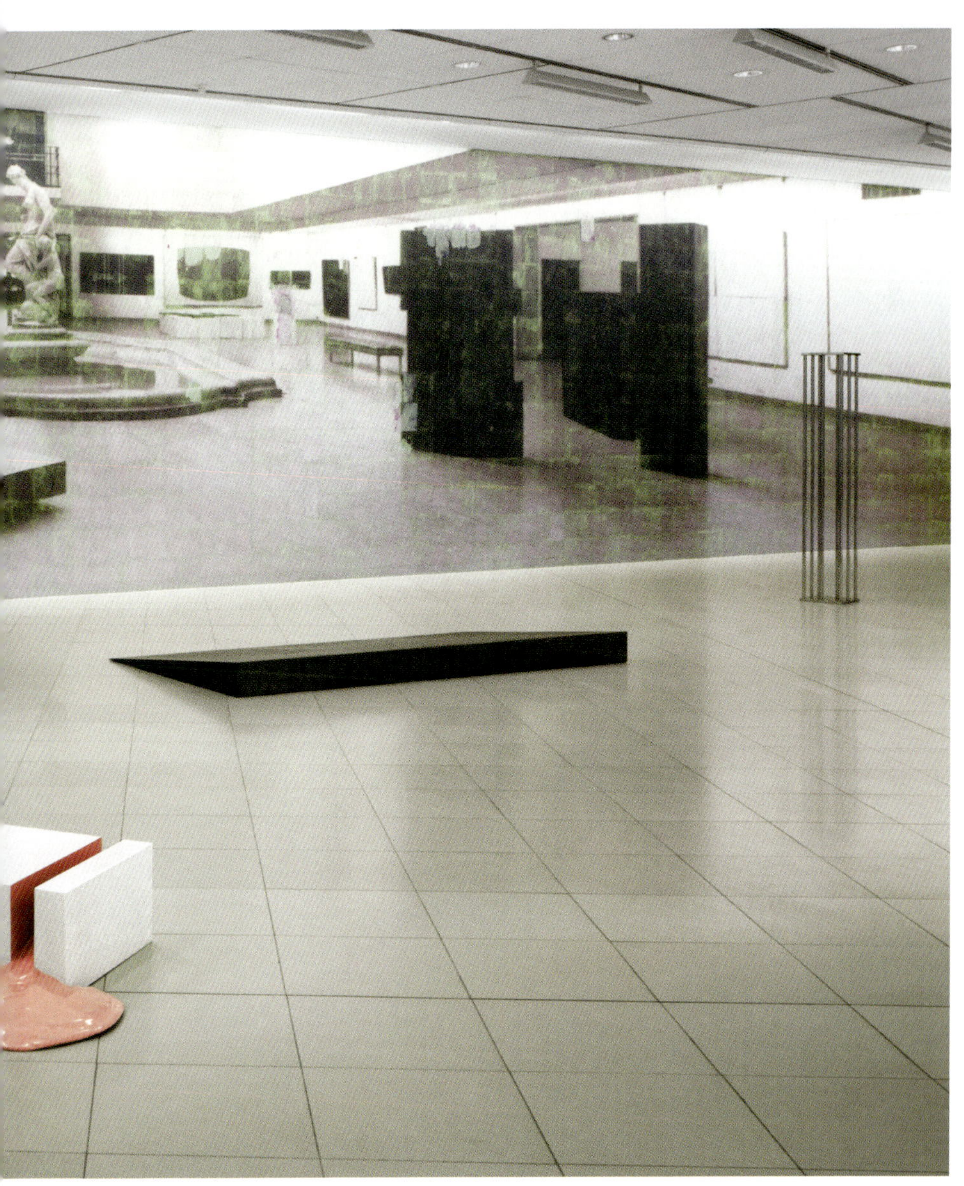

A WORK OF MANY DIMENSIONS
Simon Dybbroe Møller's <u>Black, White and Gray (Cyan, Magenta and Yellow)</u>

Lars Bang Larsen

1.

Donald Judd was not convinced of the merits of the exhibition <u>Black, White and Gray</u>. In a review he wrote of it, he opened with the salvo, "Black, white and gray, like black and white, is meager as a theme."[1] More than forty years later, Simon Dybbroe Møller would make a work to contradict the master of Minimalism – or, depending on the way you look at it, complete Judd's judgement by adding a few colours. Judd probably didn't mean to reject the tradition of monochrome painting and its utopian blueprints for tomorrow, which still held its ground at the time of his writing in the early 1960s, but he could be said to have barked up the wrong tree concerning the way information technologies as binary as black and white would come to define the future. Strictly speaking, he couldn't have known about this, though, or it wasn't in the cards of his artistic practice to take such detailed flights of futurist fancy. Simon Dybbroe Møller, on the other hand, probably wouldn't mind that we call his works time machines, seeing how their primary concern could be said to be dimensionality.

Dybbroe Møller's work <u>Black, White and Gray (Cyan, Magenta and Yellow)</u> from 2006, is a wallpaper about thirty metres long and as high as the room in which it is installed. It consists of over two thousand single sheets of standard DIN A4 paper, each of which seems

like a large pixel of a photographic image that has
been partitioned up in a grid in a computer. In
combination, the sheets of paper compose an
installation shot from the exhibition of minimal
sculpture and painting <u>Black, White and Gray</u> curated
by Samuel Wagstaff, Jr. and opened at the Atheneum
Museum in Wadsworth, Connecticut in January 1964.
<u>Black, White and Gray</u> is sometimes described as the
first Minimalist art exhibition - a debatable claim,
but it did do much in the way of promoting an austere,
minimal look to a mainstream and middlebrow audience.[II]
The image conveyed in Dybbroe Møller's wallpaper is
a composite of two installation views, put together
to convey a panorama of the exhibition's main space.
On the picture we see works by, among others, Robert
Morris, Tony Smith, Anne Truitt and James Lee Byars,
installed in the museum's atrium around a Mannerist
sculpture of the early seventeenth century by Pietro
Francavilla, <u>Venus with a Nymph and Satyr</u> (c. 1600).
    However, the wallpaper has a strange rash, as if
it were an undead picture with the face of a zombie,
or overlaid with the verdigris patina of a bronze
sculpture that has spent decades in a park. The story
is this: When Dybbroe Møller spent the summer holiday
of 2006 sailing on the Mediterranean, he carried
around with him a sheet of paper with some addresses
that he had printed out in an Internet café. When
he took the paper out of his trouser pocket after
a few days, the black letters had produced what he
calls a "psychedelic colour blur" after having been
exposed to water.[III] A similar process is deliberately
employed in <u>Black, White and Gray (Cyan, Magenta and
Yellow)</u>. All prints are black and white but printed
in the CMYK-scale, and when applied to the wall with

wallpaper paste, the chemicals and moisture of the paste separate the blue, magenta and yellow from the black ink – hence adding colours to supplement the photo's 'meagre' tones of black, white and gray. The colours appear in the gestural strokes of the glue brush by whoever pasted up the sheets. The primary structures are documented in the image under a veil of allegorical opacity.

Time machines are likewise known to produce surprising hues and tricks of the light. This is the fast-forwarded cosmic vista that H.G. Wells's time traveller beheld when he mounted his machine of nickel, ivory and rock crystal, pressed the start lever and departed for the future:

As I put on pace, night followed day like the flapping of a black wing. The dim suggestion of the laboratory seemed presently to fall away from me, and I saw the sun hopping swiftly across the sky, leaping it every minute, and every minute marking a day. I supposed the laboratory had been destroyed and I had come into the open air. I had a dim impression of scaffolding, but I was already going too fast to be conscious of any moving things. The slowest snail that ever crawled dashed by too fast for me. The twinkling succession of darkness and light was excessively painful to the eye. Then, in the intermittent darknesses, I saw the moon spinning swiftly through her quarters from new to full, and had a faint glimpse of the circling stars. Presently, as I went on, still gaining velocity, the palpitation of night and day merged into one continuous greyness; the sky took on a wonderful deepness of blue, a splendid luminous

colour like that of early twilight; the jerking
sun became a streak of fire, a brilliant arch, in
space; the moon a fainter fluctuating band; and I
could see nothing of the stars, save now and then
a brighter circle flickering in the blue.[IV]

A similar glitch in time appears in Dybbroe Møller.
The title of his 2006 solo exhibition at Künstlerhaus
Bremen, <u>Letter From the New World to the Old World</u>
(where <u>Black, White and Gray (Cyan, Magenta and
Yellow)</u> was first shown) ostensibly referred to a
letter sent from the US to Europe. But what if this
movement is temporal rather than geographic, and the
'new world' is accordingly not a different place, but
a different time? What letters would we be receiving?
His works revisit existing things with questions and
hypotheses that are different from what the present
would itself convey. This is not a healing of history,
nor is it a longing for the past. Rather, his works
make for strange images and objects that never were,
but are crystallised results of new becomings, or
monuments to possible outcomes that a common past can
yield – to things that will have been, if we follow
through on our desire for the future. They are not
about changing your past to change your future, but
about intervening in the future to change the way past
appears in the present.

It is in this kind of uncovering of the ruins of
possible tomorrows, this kind of 'archaeology of the
future', as we might say with the words of Frederic
Jameson, that I believe Dybbroe Møller is engaged.[V]
It is often said that his work is about modernism, and
it is true that this is the era he typically revisits to
find raw material. However, it seems to be modernism's

energies and its desire to conceive of the world of
tomorrow that he is mining, rather than modernism as it
actually took place. Today, in a global culture that is
mainly preoccupied with reproducing itself, the future
is as threatened a resource as oil, unspoiled nature
and clean drinking water: In view of this predicament,
Dybbroe Møller employs Modernism to look at what is
left of the future. (Artists such as David Maljkovic,
Goshka Macuga, Maria Loboda and Paul Sietsema, to name
a few from his generation, could be said to be on a
similar quest.)

2.
Through colour, <u>Black, White and Gray (Cyan,
Magenta and Yellow)</u> opens up to a kind of refracted
sedimentation, layers of history that can be peeled
back and displaced and transformed as light through a
prism. This is because colour tends to upset reality
and make reality run into other dimensions. That is,
when it isn't subsumed by an object, colour's opacity
shames language and thinking as tools with which we
nail down the real, or with which we hold fast to it.
Rendering reality soft and pliable by means of colour
was most definitely also a concern of the psychedelic
art and culture of the 1960s. And Dybbroe Møller
mentioned this aspect specifically as a reference
that may turn out to go deeper than superficial
similarities and suggest a kind of psychedelic method
at work in the installation's freeing of colour. The
day-glo colours and light shows of amorphous blobs
typical of psychedelic art and culture were a wayward,
affective vulgarisation of abstract art's universalism
that mimicked chemical transformations in the blood
stream through colour's humiliation of form. Colour

was liberated from the picture plane and turned into
a concrete yet disembodied presence in social space:
seductive and molecular, as if a spirit or a gas.
Another psychedelic reference that would be relevant to
Dybbroe Møller's piece is 'blotter art'; the miniscule
motifs to identify different trips or 'brands' that drug
entrepreneurs would ask designers to produce for the
stamp-sized blotter paper saturated with liquid LSD. As
we shall see, <u>Black, White and Gray (Cyan, Magenta and
Yellow)</u> implies Minimalist and Conceptual art in terms
of method as well as in terms of art-historical fact.
Psychedelia – bringing with it unmapped energies, as an
art-historical delinquent with baroque leanings – might
well be the third ingredient that lends Dybbroe Møller's
piece its particular dynamics. The use of colour and the
evocation of psychedelia and its mobilisation of affect
are, in any case, ironic in the context of <u>Black, White
and Gray</u> inasmuch as the exhibition was an antidote to
action painting and its "emotionalism of color", as
Wagstaff, Jr. wrote.[VI]

What, then, is the art historical narrative that
<u>Black, White and Gray (Cyan, Magenta and Yellow)</u> peels
back and refracts? It was Donald Judd's review of
<u>Black, White and Gray</u> – he was not included in the
show – as much as the exhibition itself that made it
a landmark event for Minimalist art. Amongst laconic
value judgments about the show and the art on display,
Judd formulated in the review concepts that would become
staples of Minimalist art. Hailing an art that expressed
"flat, unhierarchic, unevaluating views", he wrote that,

> A work is a familiar object or a depiction of one,
> often familiar too. It doesn't appear to be art.
> Its only claim to be is that it is being exhibited.

It is shown as art and becomes the equal of
things that are obviously art. The importance of
art is extended to everything, most of which is
slight, ordinary and unconsidered. You are forced
to consider the ordinary things and to question
whatever was thought important in art. [...]
Art could be made of any number of new objects,
materials and techniques.[VII]

For its second installation at the MMK in Frankfurt
am Main, Black, White and Gray (Cyan, Magenta and
Yellow) set the stage for a selection of works from
the MMK's collection. Two of those were in the Black,
White and Gray show: Jim Dine's Black Bathroom #1
(1962) and Andy Warhol's White Disaster II (1963).[VIII]
These works, selected by MMK director Udo Kittelmann,
brought artists from the original line-up together with
other canonical post-war North Americans related to
Minimalist, geometric and non-compositional practices:
apart from Dine and Warhol, Jo Baer, Donald Judd, Gary
Kuehn, Walter De Maria, Bruce Nauman, Robert Morris,
Robert Ryman and Cy Twombly. With Black, White and Gray
(Cyan, Magenta and Yellow) as a backdrop - historically
as well as physically looming, but reduced to two
dimensions -, these works leapt back to life from the
archive, as if they had been taken out of the picture,
their immediate presence delayed by forty-three years.
    Few of the selected works at the MMK represent
uncompromising Minimalism: Perhaps only Walter De
Maria's slick and narrow Cage (1965), the three Judds
(two 'shelves', as one might refer to them, and a floor
piece consisting of a black cuneiform metal slab), and
the one woman in the selection, Jo Baer (with a diptych
of monochrome, white canvases with painted black

frames – quite literally a hard-edge piece), could be
referred to in this way. Quite a few of the other works
embody narrative and reductive impulses on a collision
course, for example Bruce Nauman's 1968 video <u>From
Flesh to White to Black to Flesh</u>, in which the artist
applies and removes white and black pigment to his
torso, or Robert Morris's <u>Fountain</u> (1963), a galvanised
bucket hanging on a hook, from which emanates not the
sound of its own making, but that of running water.
A literalist pun on Duchamp, no doubt, which – in the
context of Dybbroe Møller's piece – also comes to refer
to the Mannerist fountain in the photo. Other works
bring quasi-pictorialist goofiness to the fore, such
as Gary Kuehn's <u>Practitioner's Delight</u> (1966), a white
rectangle on the floor that has apparently been sliced
at one end to make the 'filling' – a shiny pink puddle
cast in plastic – spill out: Minimalism good enough
to eat, and corresponding with the uninvited pink
protruding from Dybbroe Møller's piece in places where
the wallpaper paste has been heavily applied. Robert
Ryman chips in with grungy materiality in a white
monochrome (<u>Adelphi</u>, 1967).

The works in the installation shot from the
Atheneum are obviously folded back into two dimensions.
But the dimensional reduction of <u>Black, White and
Gray (Cyan, Magenta and Yellow)</u> is only apparent. By
performing a series of contradictory movements, the
work is an exploration of an art-historical document
and attains a layered dynamic. One expression of this
dimensional tension is the struggle between painting
and sculpture that, throughout Modernism, was a charged
territory for ambitious art that actualised space
(and that was also on the agenda of <u>Black, White and
Gray</u>, if only implicitly, by dint of all the works

in the show being in these two categories). At the
same time, the depicted space is not only represented
once (that is, photographically), but twice, as it is
enlarged to life size, or l a r g e r than life size.
Secondly, Dybbroe Møller stays true to Minimalism by
working within a grid system and by using materials
that are inherently loaded with meaning; in this case
ironically so, as the material loaded with meaning
turns out to be the black ink containing the colours
that the exhibition Black, White and Gray repressed
in its reduction of visual incident. This multilayered
revisitation of the Minimalist heritage makes Black,
White and Gray (Cyan, Magenta and Yellow) as bombastic
as an Anselm Kiefer and as ephemeral and fragile as a
Gustaf Metzger.

The latter reference points to tensions within
Minimalism itself: on the one hand its transcendental
vectors of 'unhierarchic, unevaluating' views, on
the other hand its insistence on a t t i t u d e ,
which presumes interest or intentionality (both Judd
and Wagstaff evoke art's new 'attitude' in their
discussions of Black, White and Gray). At the same
time, Minimalism's critics - with Michael Fried as the
most notable amongst them - are likewise challenged
by Dybbroe Møller's work. Fried's late modernist
emphasis on 'opticality' as a precondition for the
disembodied experience of the fully present art object
undergoes a paradoxical twist in Black, White and
Gray (Cyan, Magenta and Yellow), as it is the work's
opticality, its weird visuality, - perhaps more than
its size - that makes it such a visceral piece: The
image's apparent corrosion turns it into a living
being. In this way, the art-historical moorings of both
Minimalism and its critique are cut loose, setting it

afloat again within the present. You could say that
the work repotentialises a historical art form by
intervening in the disciplinary infrastructure that
has been used to write its history: the museum and its
archival methods.

3.
Other works of Dybbroe Møller's are photographic, but
<u>Black, White and Gray (Cyan, Magenta and Yellow)</u> works
through photography as a temporal device in a special
way. The process of 'developing' the black-and-white
prints with paper glue makes for a strange afterimage
of the original photo. This is compounded by the way
the piece has been produced using what appears to be a
simple desktop printing method; xeroxing, essentially,
which is a photographic medium, and one that moreover
is a p r o j e c t i v e procedure - with all this
implies for future activity - because of its capacity
to generate unities that are identical to the model.
At the end of the 1960s, a cheaper, faster and more
democratic approach to art-making was inconceivable.
As Marshall McLuhan wrote in 1967,

> Xerography - every man's brain picker - heralds
> the time of instant publishing. Anybody can now
> become both author and publisher. Take any book on
> any subject and custom-make your own book simply
> by Xeroxing a chapter from this one, a chapter
> from that one - instant steal![IX]

Today, of course, photocopying and desktop printing
are unbelievably mundane procedures of reproducibility
(to which McLuhan applied the rather more exciting
term 'stealing'). In the context of <u>Black, White</u>

and Gray (Cyan, Magenta and Yellow), it makes for an approach that, in its poor and reduced anti-formalism, is closer to Conceptualism than to Minimalism's representation-as-realisation. This brings to mind how the first generation of New York Conceptualists were of the opinion that Minimalist artists had not carried their own principles of a separation of material and idea to a logical conclusion.

The conventional mistrust of photography as art is that it is not original - that it is a (photo)copy. Another, more sinister, reality of the photographic image is that it is arrested time in which the dead look back at us, as Roland Barthes put it. In the photo of the Wadsworth Atheneum it is not only the minimal works that are looking back at us, but also Francavilla's venus: a mythological female presence that beholds us across the centuries from Mannerism, the artistic movement that marked the first time art became aware of itself as art. The sculpture's opulence underscores the look of elegant refusal of the mid-twentieth-century works that surround it in the picture.

Dybbroe Møller's work is an image as visually puzzling as it is physically engaging: combined of two originals, enlarged, cut into little pieces, and corroded, the double-edged temporality of a scene that is as deep as four hundred years of art history and as flat as a photocopy, folded back onto itself with an artificial patina. They say that psychics see the dead not as pallid ghosts but as coloured spots or blurred absences in space. When we start moving about in time, we can perhaps expect to behold something similar to when we move in the other dimensions of space: continuous grayness, or splendid luminous colour, as

H.G. Wells described it. <u>Black, White and Gray (Cyan, Magenta and Yellow)</u> is a picture of a faded pantheon that looks totally exhausted, irremediably relegated to the archive but, like some bleeding icon of a saint, proves that it is alive by oozing colour. But its 'bleeding' is profane rather than transcendental, as it is the effect that brings the photo back from trans-historical space to the here and now.

Perhaps Dybbroe Møller's use of colour ultimately allegorises two things: Firstly, the tendency of historical categorisation to package artistic phenomena and art history through narratives that emblematise the art they take as their object at the risk of excluding works that are empirically relevant but don't fit the bill. A quite literal example of this forcing of the narrative was the way Wagstaff tried to persuade Warhol to produce a set of white <u>Brillo</u> boxes for the <u>Black, White and Gray</u> show, seeing how the original <u>Brillos</u> in red and blue didn't fit the bill. As the art historian James Meyer dryly notes, "Warhol ended up sending two <u>White Disasters</u> instead."[x] And whoever heard of the cement <u>Pizza</u> and <u>Dog Turd</u> sculptures Carl Andre produced in the early '60s? Why did we never read about those? Pizzas and dog turds – flat, unhierarchic, unevaluating art works indeed, but nonetheless conveniently filtered out in most accounts of Minimal art.

Secondly, colour in <u>Black, White and Gray (Cyan, Magenta and Yellow)</u> allegorises the way the reception of a work or an exhibition always exceeds artistic intention and discussion and makes art and its surrounding social space bleed into each other in unexpected ways. According to the style-conscious Samuel Wagstaff, Jr., for <u>Black, White and Gray</u> this was exemplified by the way the exhibition made "a terrific hit" with the editors of <u>Vogue</u> magazine, who devoted a six-page spread to it. Entitled <u>Fascinating this minute: black-and-white excitement is back</u>, the magazine's coverage of the show featured, among other items, a photo of a swan-necked model with a gravity-defying coiffure, poised in front of Morris's <u>Untitled (Column)</u> and <u>Untitled (Slab)</u> and wearing a tapered gown in... pink.[XI]

^I Donald Judd, "Black, White and Gray", in: <u>Arts Magazine</u>, New York, March 1964, pp. 117-19, 117.

^{II} See James Meyer's account of the show in: <u>Minimalism. Art and Polemics in the Sixties</u>, New Haven: Yale University Press, 2004 (2001), pp. 76-81.

^{III} Simon Dybbroe Møller in an e-mail to the author, July 3, 2008 (translation from Dutch by the author).

^{IV} Herbert G. Wells, <u>The Time Machine</u>, London: Penguin Classics, 2005 (1895), p. 19.

^V See Frederic Jameson, <u>Archaeologies of the Future</u>, London: Verso, 2005.

^{VI} See Meyer, p. 77.

^{VII} Judd, p. 118.

^{VIII} It was about Warhol that Judd, in his review, rather sweetly said that "at heart he's an Expressionist" (see Judd, p. 119), an epithet that must have encouraged Warhol to adjust his professional profile.

^{IX} Marshall McLuhan and Quentin Fiore: <u>The Medium is the Massage</u>, London: Penguin Books, 1967, p. 125.

^X Meyer, p. 78.

^{XI} Ibid.

Werkliste / List of works

S. / p. 34-35, 38-39, 42-43, Umschlag / cover
Simon Dybbroe Møller (*1976)
Black, White and Gray (Cyan, Magenta and Yellow), 2006
Inkjet-Ausdrucke auf DIN-A4-Papier, Tapetenkleister /
inkjet prints on DIN A4 paper, wallpaper paste

Museum für Moderne Kunst, Frankfurt am Main
Erworben mit großzügiger Unterstützung der Partner des Museum für
Moderne Kunst / acquired with generous support of the partners of the
Museum für Moderne Kunst: DekaBank Deutsche Girozentrale, DELTON AG,
Deutsche Bank AG, Eurohypo AG, Helaba Landesbank Hessen-Thüringen,
KfW Bankengruppe & UBS Deutschland AG

S. / p. 7
Donald Judd (1928-1994)
Untitled, 1965/68
Perforierter, kaltgewalzter Stahl / perforated, cold-rolled steel
167,6 x 304,8 x 20,3 cm

Museum für Moderne Kunst, Frankfurt am Main
Ehemalig / previously: Sammlung Karl Ströher, Darmstadt

S. / p. 9
Walter De Maria (*1935)
Pyramid Chair, 1966
V-Stahl, verchromt, Lackleder, Stahlblech, Kunstharzlack /
v-steel, chromed, patent leather, sheet steel, synthetic enamel
218,7 x 127,7 x 87,6 cm

Museum für Moderne Kunst, Frankfurt am Main
Ehemalig / previously: Sammlung Karl Ströher, Darmstadt

S. / p. 11
Jim Dine (*1935)
Black Bathroom #1, 1962
Öl auf Nessel, Spiegelschrank, Seifenablage, Becherhalter, Wasserhahn /
oil on nettle, mirror cabinet, soap dish, beaker holder, water tap
189 x 186 x 17 cm

Museum für Moderne Kunst, Frankfurt am Main
Ehemalig / previously: Sammlung Karl Ströher, Darmstadt

S. / p. 13
Bruce Nauman (*1941)
From Flesh to White to Black to Flesh, 1968
Video, 30 min

Museum für Moderne Kunst, Frankfurt am Main

S. / p. 15
Gary Kuehn (*1939)
Black Painting, 1972
Acryl auf Leinwand / acrylic on canvas
95,5 x 141 cm

Museum für Moderne Kunst, Frankfurt am Main
Erworben mit großzügiger Unterstützung der Partner des Museum für
Moderne Kunst / acquired with generous support of the partners of the
Museum für Moderne Kunst: DekaBank Deutsche Girozentrale, DELTON AG,
Deutsche Bank AG, Eurohypo AG, Helaba Landesbank Hessen-Thüringen,
KfW Bankengruppe & UBS Deutschland AG

S. / p. 17
Robert Morris (*1931)
Fountain, 1963
Zinkeimer, Holzbalken bemalt, Eisenhaken, Elektropumpe, Wasser /
zinc bucket, painted wood truss, iron hook, electric pump, water
91 x 32 x 37 cm

Museum für Moderne Kunst, Frankfurt am Main
Ehemalig / previously: Sammlung Karl Ströher, Darmstadt

S. / p. 19
Donald Judd (*1928)
<u>Untitled (#94, 1967)</u>, 1988
Verzinktes Eisen / galvanized iron
12,7 x 183 x 21,8 cm

Kunstmuseum, St. Gallen
Ehemalig / previously: Sammlung Rolf Ricke im / at
Kunstmuseum, St. Gallen, Kunstmuseum Liechtenstein, Vaduz &
Museum für Moderne Kunst, Frankfurt am Main

S. / p. 21
Gary Kuehn (*1939)
<u>Practitioner's Delight</u>, 1966
Metall, Kunstharz, Fiberglas, lackiert /
metal, synthetic resin, fibreglass, varnished
30,4 x 142,2 x 99,3 cm

Museum für Moderne Kunst, Frankfurt am Main
Ehemalig / previously: Sammlung Rolf Ricke im / at
Museum für Moderne Kunst, Frankfurt am Main,
Kunstmuseum, St. Gallen & Kunstmuseum Liechtenstein, Vaduz

S. / p. 23
Jo Baer (*1929)
<u>Ohne Titel (Diptych)</u>, 1966-70
Öl und Acrylfarbe auf Leinwand / oil and acrylic on canvas
Jeweils / each 182,9 x 132 cm

Museum für Moderne Kunst, Frankfurt am Main
Ehemalig / previously: Sammlung Rolf Ricke im / at
Museum für Moderne Kunst, Frankfurt am Main,
Kunstmuseum, St. Gallen & Kunstmuseum Liechtenstein, Vaduz

S. / p. 25
Cy Twombly (*1928)
<u>Problem I, II, III</u>, 1966
Tempera und Kreide auf industriell grundierter Leinwand /
tempera and chalk on industrially undercoated canvas
200 x 108 x 9 cm, 200 x 112 x 2,5 cm, 200 x 112 x 2,5 cm

Museum für Moderne Kunst, Frankfurt am Main
Ehemalig / previously: Sammlung Karl Ströher, Darmstadt

S. / p. 27
Walter De Maria (*1935)
Cage, 1965
V-Stahl, poliert / v-steel, polished
216,5 x 37 x 37 cm

Museum für Moderne Kunst, Frankfurt am Main
Ehemalig / previously: Sammlung Karl Ströher, Darmstadt

S. / p. 29
Andy Warhol (*1928)
White Disaster II (White Burning Car II), 1963
Siebdruckfarbe auf Leinwand / screenprint on canvas
269,5 x 208,3 cm

Museum für Moderne Kunst, Frankfurt am Main
Ehemalig / previously: Sammlung Karl Ströher, Darmstadt

S. / p. 31
Donald Judd (1928-1994)
Untitled, 1987
Aluminium, einbrennlackiert / aluminium, stove-enamelled
30 x 150 x 30 cm

Kunstmuseum Liechtenstein, Vaduz
Ehemalig / previously: Sammlung Rolf Ricke im / at
Kunstmuseum Liechtenstein, Vaduz,
Museum für Moderne Kunst, Frankfurt am Main &
Kunstmuseum, St. Gallen

S. / p. 33
Robert Ryman (*1930)
Adelphi, 1967
Öl auf Leinwand, Pergamentpapier, Tesakrepp /
oil on canvas, vellum paper, masking tape
258 x 258 cm

Museum für Moderne Kunst, Frankfurt am Main
Ehemalig / previously: Sammlung Karl Ströher, Darmstadt

Die Publikation Black, White, Gray, Cyan, Magenta, Yellow
von Simon Dybbroe Møller ist kein Ausstellungskatalog
im üblichen Sinne, sondern vielmehr ein vom Künstler
konzipiertes Buch. Im seinem Zentrum steht Dybbroe Møllers
Arbeit Black, White and Gray (Cyan, Magenta and Yellow)
von 2006, die im Rahmen der Ausstellung Das Kapital.
Blue Chips & Masterpieces im MMK Museum für Moderne Kunst
vom 20. April bis 26. August 2007 zu sehen war und für
die Sammlung angekauft wurde. Das Kapital. Blue Chips &
Masterpieces zeigte herausragende Arbeiten des MMK in
ihrem ersten Dialog mit den Werken der Sammlung Rolf
Ricke, der umfangreichsten und wertvollsten Erwerbung
von Arbeiten, die das MMK seit dem Ankauf der Sammlung
Karl Ströher 1981 tätigte. Das Buch zeigt die besondere
Eingliederung der Arbeit Dybbroe Møllers in die ›alte‹ und
›neue‹ Sammlung des MMK.

The publication Black, White, Gray, Cyan, Magenta, Yellow
by Simon Dybbroe Møller is not an exhibition catalogue
in the strict sense, but rather a book conceived by the
artist. It is centered around Dybbroe Møller's work Black,
White and Gray (Cyan, Magenta and Yellow) from 2006, which
was shown as part of the exhibition Das Kapital. Blue
Chips & Masterpieces at the MMK Museum für Moderne Kunst
from April 20 to August 26, 2007 and was acquired for
the collection. Das Kapital. Blue Chips & Masterpieces
showcased outstanding works from the MMK collection in
their first dialogue with the œuvres from the Rolf Ricke
Collection, the most extensive and valuabele acquisition
made by the MMK since the purchase of the Karl Ströher
Collection in 1981. The book illustrates the way in which
Dybbroe Møller's work integrates itself into the 'old' and
'new' collection of the MMK.

Impressum / Imprint

Herausgeber / editor: Udo Kittelmann, MMK Museum für Moderne Kunst, Frankfurt am Main

Konzept / concept: Simon Dybbroe Møller & Karsten Heller

Redaktion / editing: Dorothée Brill

Übersetzung aus dem Englischen / translation from English: Benjamin Meyer-Krahmer

Lektorat / proof-reading: Helga Ostermeier, Judith Rosenthal, Kinga Wiglusch

Fotografien / photographs: Axel Schneider

Gestaltung / design: DiG Berlin

Lithographie / lithography: Max Color

Herstellung / production: Medialis

Umschlag / cover:
Simon Dybbroe Møller, <u>Black, White and Gray (Cyan, Magenta and Yellow)</u>, 2006 (Ausschnitt / detail)

Verlag / publisher

Verlag der Buchhandlung Walther König, Köln
Ehrenstr. 4, 50672 Köln
Tel +49 (0)221 20 596 53
Fax +49 (0)221 20 596 60
E-mail: verlag@buchhandlung-walther-koenig.de

Die Deutsche Bibliothek - CIP-Einheitsaufnahme
Ein Titelsatz für diese Publikation ist
bei der Deutschen Bibliothek erhältlich
Printed in Germany

Vertrieb / distribution

Schweiz / Switzerland:
Buch 2000
c/o AVA, Verlagsauslieferungen AG
Centralweg 16, Postfach 27
CH-8910 Affoltern a.A.
Tel +41 (0)1 762 42 00
Fax +41 (0)1 762 42 10
a.koll@ava.ch

Großbritannien und Irland / UK and Ireland:
Cornerhouse Publications
70 Oxford Street
GB-Manchester M1 5NH
Tel +44 (0)161 200 15 03
Fax +44 (0)161 200 15 04
publications@cornerhouse.org

Außerhalb Europas / outside Europe:
D.A.P / Distributed Art Publishers, Inc.
155 6th Avenue, 2nd Floor
New York, NY 10013
Tel +1 (0)212 627 1999
Fax +1 (0)212 627 9484

ISBN 978-3-86560-571-9